THE ILLUSTRATED HISTORY OF
SEAPLANES AND
FLYING BOATS

THE ILLUSTRATED HISTORY OF
SEAPLANES
AND
FLYING BOATS

LOUIS S CASEY AND JOHN BATCHELOR

Hamlyn
LONDON · NEW YORK · SYDNEY · TORONTO
in association with Phoebus

CONTENTS

Previous page: A New York, Rio and Buenos Aires Line Consolidated Commodore banks low over the Statue of Liberty

Left: Lieutenant GD Cuddihy USN with an R3C-2 in the days when pilots did not need a G suit or wear fire resistant overalls and a flying helmet with built in microphone and head set. This Curtiss racer, first built as the R3C-1 with a wheeled undercarriage, became the R3C-2 when it was fitted with floats for the Schneider Trophy

Published by the Hamlyn Publishing Group Limited
London · New York · Sydney · Toronto
Astronaut House, Feltham, Middlesex, England

This edition © 1980 Phoebus Publishing Company/BPC Publishing Company Limited
52 Poland Street, London W1A 2JX

This material first appeared in *Floatplanes and Racers* © 1979 Phoebus Publishing Co/BPC Publishing Ltd; *Seaplanes and Flying Boats* © 1979 Phoebus Publishing Co/BPC Publishing Ltd

ISBN 0 600 38259 1

Printed in Great Britain by Redwood Burn Limited, Trowbridge, Wiltshire

INTRODUCTION

Water was popular with early aviators, as it has not only a soft surface but can offer an almost unlimited area for lumbering take-offs by primitive aircraft. Hence early floatplanes and flying boats were used in the air races before and after World War I. During the war they became a vital part of the coastal patrols of the combatant nations.

The Schneider Trophy of the 1920s and 1930s became the incentive for developing some of the most attractive single-seat floatplanes ever designed, but it also allowed aircraft designers to produce engines which were to receive their ultimate test during the coming war.

World War II was the heyday of the flying boat and floatplane. They had a vital role in the massive naval battles in the Pacific and played a major part in crushing the German U-Boat campaign.

Since the war, floatplanes have remained popular especially in the remote areas of Finland, North and South America and Australasia where water is plentiful and landing strips limited. Flying boats are still in service with a few military operators, but they are most well known for their work as fire-fighters. Water bombers have the ability to scoop up gallons of water and then fly to remote locations and 'bomb' the fire.

Seaplanes and flying boats have had an important part to play in peace and war since men first took to the air. This book tells their story.

A Curtiss A-1 at Hammondsport in 1911. Lieutenant Ellyson is at the controls with Captain Chambers as a prudent passenger with a kapok float. Chambers flew as a passenger three times in the A-1 while Lieutenant Ellyson has the distinction of being listed as the first US Navy pilot

PART I

FLOATPLANES

AND

RACERS

US Navy and Marine officers with their maintenance crew pose in front of a NAF PT-1. For all their glamour, pilots were completely dependent on the men sitting and standing around them

THE FIRST SEAPLANES

The first aircraft to take off from water was the Gnome-powered floatplane of Henri Fabre, on 28 March 1910, at Martigues, France. By September that year, Fabre had succeeded in making flights for a distance of up to 2 miles (3 km). Unfortunately, Fabre did not continue with his experiments and did not produce a commercial successor to this first hydro. Consequently, his name is all but forgotten in the annals of aviation.

The second and, historically, the most important step in water-based flying occurred with the development by Glenn H Curtiss of the first successful hydro aircraft in the United States. After numerous experiments, which began with the Aerial Experiment Association's Loon in 1908, Curtiss was able to make the first public flight in North America at North Island, San Diego, California, on 26 January, 1911, when he piloted a modified Curtiss Model D aircraft. The Loon was, in fact, the modified version of the AEA June Bug in which Curtiss had won the Scientific American Trophy for the first time on 4 July, 1908.

During the period when the AEA Silver Dart was under construction, a pair of floats was built and mounted, catamaran fashion, under the June Bug. The engine intended for the Silver Dart was requisitioned and installed in the machine which was then called the Loon. Viewed with the hindsight of 70 years, it was virtually impossible that the Loon could ever have risen from the surface of Lake Keuka at Hammondsport, New York. The engine, which was estimated to produce only 20-30 hp, coupled with the flat bottom-surface of the triangular cross-section floats, doomed the experiment before it had even started. If this was not enough, the sternpost of one of the floats was torn loose as the Loon taxied away from the dock, causing the float to leak. Repeated runs up and down the lake failed to get the Loon clear of the water. Although it did plane on the flat-bottom surfaces of the floats, it failed to get 'unstuck'.

Another early and unsuccessful attempt was the 1908 Blériot hydro, whose almost comic gyrations were the first recorded on motion picture (cinema) film as it cavorted along the Seine, towed by the motor boat *La Rapière*.

Following the Loon failures, Curtiss continued to experiment with water-based aircraft after the dissolution of the AEA. In May 1909, Curtiss built his own concept of a single-float configuration, which was discussed in the Bulletins of the AEA.

Curtiss mounted a standard Curtiss Model D airframe on a conventional canoe, which was decked over with doped canvas, to test his single-float theory as opposed to the double-float catamaran configuration. Curtiss compared the single-float controllability and general handling characteristics to those of a bicycle. He explained in the AEA Bulletin that the single-float improved handling on the water. He added that if one float was damaged, as had happened with the Loon, the lateral balance would not be altered to the detriment of the aircraft.

The Curtiss experiments continued, based on a crude float system similar to the Fabre float design. By cut-and-try extensions to the main supporting float, Curtiss was able to effect a take-off several days before the first public demonstration on 26 January, 1911. At the time of the demonstration, his Model D had a broad-beamed, scow-

A small boy watches fascinated
as the Loon is readied for an
attempt at take-off. The Silver
Dart engine was only 20-30 hp
and the floats flat-bottomed
which made take-off
impossible

Glenn H Curtiss at the controls
of A-1 'Lizzie'. What she lacked
in pilot comfort she made up in
simplicity. Curtiss may have
suffered from spray and
slipstream, but he had none of
the bewildering instruments
found in modern aircraft

THE CURTISS TRIAD or A-1, 1911

A year later it set a world
seaplane altitude record of
274 m (900 ft). The type served
as a floatplane with the US
Navy and as a land aircraft with
the US Army. The dozen
aircraft with the US Navy were
given the designation AH
(airplane hydro), while the
Army received Type E aircraft

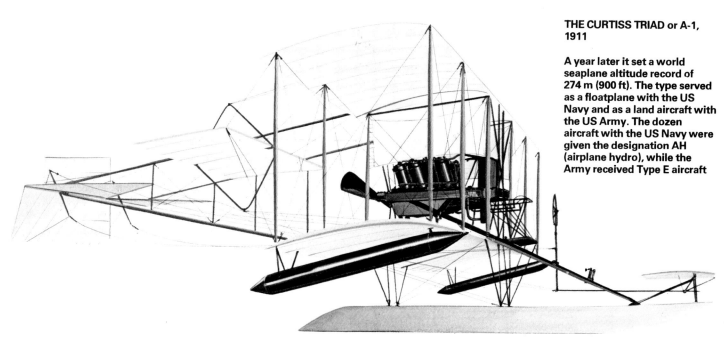

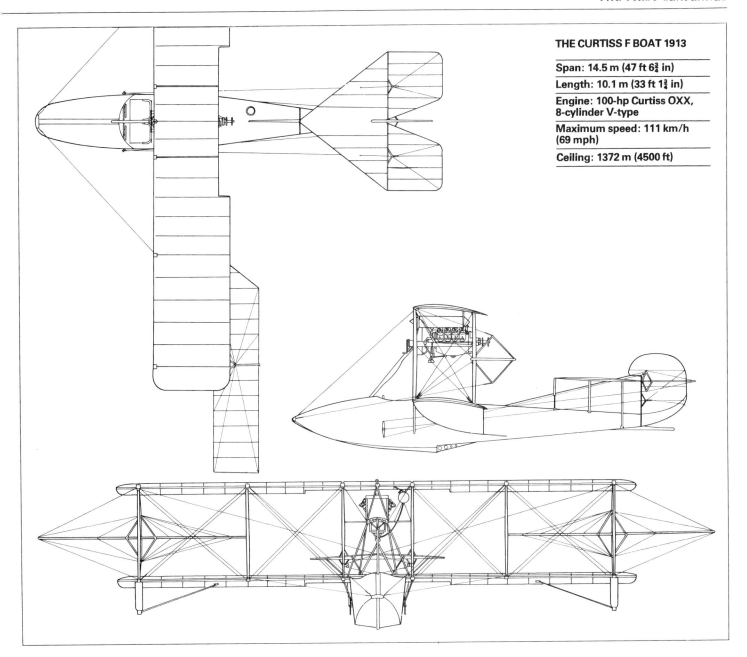

THE CURTISS F BOAT 1913

Span: 14.5 m (47 ft 6¾ in)

Length: 10.1 m (33 ft 1¾ in)

Engine: 100-hp Curtiss OXX, 8-cylinder V-type

Maximum speed: 111 km/h (69 mph)

Ceiling: 1372 m (4500 ft)

type main float, attached at the location of the rear main wheels. A second, smaller, scow-type float was fitted to the front wheel fixture. Forward of this float, a hydrofoil was fitted to prevent the front float from 'digging in' to the water when thrust was applied by the pusher propeller.

Shortly after this historic flight, the single main float was changed to a long, narrow, scow-type float, approximately 12 ft (3.66 m) long, which replaced the tandem floats. At rest on the water, and until aileron control speed was achieved, balance was maintained by two floats which were fitted under the wing tips to provide the necessary lateral support. Initially, these floats were made from motorcycle inner tubes bound to a shingle-like planing board which was mounted under each wing tip to trail at approximately a 45° angle. These crude floats were eventually replaced by canister-type floats with cone-shaped ends and, finally, in the US Navy's AH-8 aircraft, they became attractive as well as functional plywood floats.

Shortly after Curtiss made these first trial flights, he had an accident, in May 1911, which was to establish another basic construction feature of float design. While flying from Lake Keuka, Curtiss's Model D single-float hydro had sprung a leak, allowing several gallons of water to enter the float. The added weight was not sufficient to prevent take-off but, when he lowered the nose preparatory to making a landing, the water inside the float rushed to the forward end causing the plane to dive into the lake. Curtiss was thrown clear, with minor injuries, but the aircraft was a total loss. Following this accident, all floats and, later, all flying-boat hulls, were constructed with water-tight bulkheads which divided the float or flying-boat hull into multiple compartments. The size of these compartments was usually calculated to enable any two compartments to keep the plane afloat in case of a similar accident.

With the approach of winter, and lower temperatures, efforts were made to enclose the pilot to protect him from the cold wind and water spray. The first attempt was with the Curtiss E (Navy A-2) aircraft, which was modified to place the pilot lower down on the float. A framework was constructed from the bow back to the pilot's position, over which a fabric wind screen was stretched and treated with dope. The float remained basically the same, producing a bobtail appearance resembling the later 'bat boats'. In a practical sense, the A-2 had the same characteristics as the Standard E Hydro. The later addition of wheels set into pockets in the hull bottom produced what appeared to be

Right: Lieutenant Ellyson sits at the controls of a Curtiss E Flying Fish in 1912. The pilot's position has been enclosed, but elevators are still fitted in the bow position

A Curtiss AH-18 (N6 type) in 1915 at Pensacola as a training aircraft with the US Navy. The practice of using obsolescent types for trainers was common up to the late 1930s

one of the earliest attempts at amphibian aircraft, known as the OWL (over water or land). The Curtiss Triad was probably the first real amphibian, although it was nothing like the refined machine that we see in today's amphibians or triphibians (air, land and water).

The first Curtiss flying boat was under development at about the same time but due to the placement of the OX engine down in the bow of the hull and the unreliability of its chain-driven propellers, which were laterally disposed, as was the Wright brothers' propulsion system, the first Curtiss flying boat did not fly. This unsuccessful attempt was followed by a number of experiments which finally bore fruit in the form of the 1912 E Flying Fish, which was marginally successful and marked the beginning of the practical flying boat. Curtiss applied for and received basic patents covering the features of this flying boat.

The first military hydro aircraft, the Curtiss A-1, was delivered to the US Navy in 1911 and was followed shortly thereafter by the A-2/OWL (referred to earlier). These

were both Curtiss Model Es, developed from the earlier Model D Triad which had also demonstrated its capability as an amphibious floatplane at Coronado, California. Although the A-1 and the succeeding A-2 were delivered to the US Navy with optional wheel-type landing gear, in addition to the float gear, they were not routinely operated with the retractable wheels. These first naval aircraft were standard land-plane types fitted with a single central float and the smaller wing-tip, canister-shaped floats for stabilization. This single-main-float configuration was to be a standard design for the US Navy until the floatplanes were phased out of service use at the end of World War II. The twin-float configuration has been the standard, with few exceptions, for service aircraft of most other nations as well as the vast majority of civilian floatplanes. Most float aircraft, known in the early days as hydro-aeroplanes, were standard land-planes, modified by the addition of floats.

Generally, aircraft which were manufactured with the provision of float-mounting hardware were also given

Aquatic onlookers gather to
examine a Wright B-1 in
Baltimore harbour. The B-1 was
the third aircraft purchased by
the US Navy. The sailors in
summer whites are positioned
on the aircraft to keep it stable
in the water

special rust-preventative treatment during manufacture.
The special treatment was applied to the propeller also, for
it was always subject to the destructive erosion of water
thrown up over the bow of the float or the hull. As the hull
design progressed, spray strips were added or hull-bottom
contours were designed to deflect the spray pattern away
from the propeller(s).

The early period of floatplane development was characterized by aircraft which were variations of the box-kite
configuration. This period extended to the end of 1915 or
the early stages of World War I. The first British floatplane
success was the Gonsspelius monoplane, which made a
number of short experimental flights over Windermere in
1911. Like the developed Curtiss hydro, this aircraft
adopted the single-float configuration, although it differed

in shape; the Gonsspelius float was a broad-beam scow
configuration rather than the long, narrow beam of the
Curtiss float.

Commander Schwann, RN, is credited with having
developed the first successful twin-float configuration, the
35-hp Avro, flown by Sippe at Barrow-in-Furness. It can be
regarded as the successful prototype of the vast numbers
of twin-float aircraft to follow.

The year 1912 brought a number of variations on
floatplane design. The first successful monoplane floatplane was the little 80-hp Borel. A number were purchased
by the British Royal Naval Air Service as trainers but their
limited performance did not justify repeat orders.

Other manufacturers tried a variety of floats. Almost
without exception, these early floats were of the scow, flat-

THE HULL CONFIGURATIONS OF EARLY SEAPLANES

The distinction between floatplane and flying boat had not been clearly defined before World War I. It was only after a memo from the Admiralty that the navy listed seaplanes according to whether they landed on a float or floats independent from the hull, or whether the hull itself was built in a boat configuration and rested on the water – making them flying boats. Most of the types shown here are powered by pusher engines and have hulls which vary from the slim Burgess Navy type to the bulky Walco

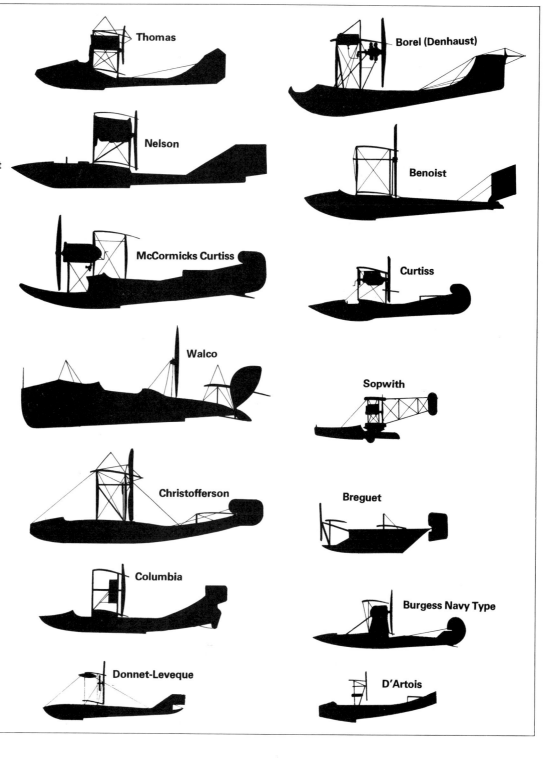

bottom, configuration and were mounted on airframes which were the standard land-plane design of the manufacturing company. Most of these were best for lake operation only, since the scow configuration was not very suitable for sea conditions greater than a choppy surface. Among the manufacturers who tried their hand with seaplanes were Brown (UK); Nieuport (France); Voisin (France) using Fabre-style floats; Short (UK); Sanchez-Besa; Grandjean (France); Farman (France); Train, Goupy (France); Aviatik (Germany); Astra; REP (France); Caudron (France); AGO, AEK, and Dr Hubner (Germany). This was quite a representation of the aircraft builders of the day – few remained beyond World War I.

The 1912 Short hydros were adaptions of standard land-planes. Short experimented with both the single-float and twin-float configurations. Gradually, they favoured the twin-float configuration, discarding the single-float design. On the other hand, Curtiss became even more committed to the single-float design. Success at home with sales to the US Navy as well as sales to the Russian and Japanese navies further confirmed the operational advantages of a single main float for naval operations.

It was also in the year 1912 that the Guidoni (Italy) monoplane was built and flown. Two years later this aircraft was to make history by experimentally dropping the first torpedo. It was quite an accomplishment, by any standard, and the forerunner of a whole branch of naval aircraft development and armament.

The Guidoni was a large machine, with a span of 66 ft (20.1 m) and a length of 50 ft (15.2 m). It weighed 6600 lb

Scenes at the Schneider Cup race meeting at Monte Carlo in 1913.
Top: A Maurice Farman floatplane. The type was used in World War I by the British, Belgians, Italians and Russians but not by the French
Centre: The Breguet entry with its typical tadpole fuselage. It proved an excellent aircraft and won the trophy that year
Bottom: The Astra entry is towed out into open water for a take-off run. Like other aircraft of the period it had flat-bottomed floats

SHORT SEAPLANE 827

The Short Admiralty Type 827 was ordered for the RNAS in the summer of 1914 and remained in service until 1918

Span: 16.43 m (53 ft 11 in) top, 12.19 m (40 ft) lower	
Length: 10.74 m (35 ft 3 in)	
Engine: 150-hp Sunbeam Nubian	
Max speed: 98.17 km/h (61 mph)	
Endurance: 3½ hr	
Armament: Bombs and Lewis machine-gun	

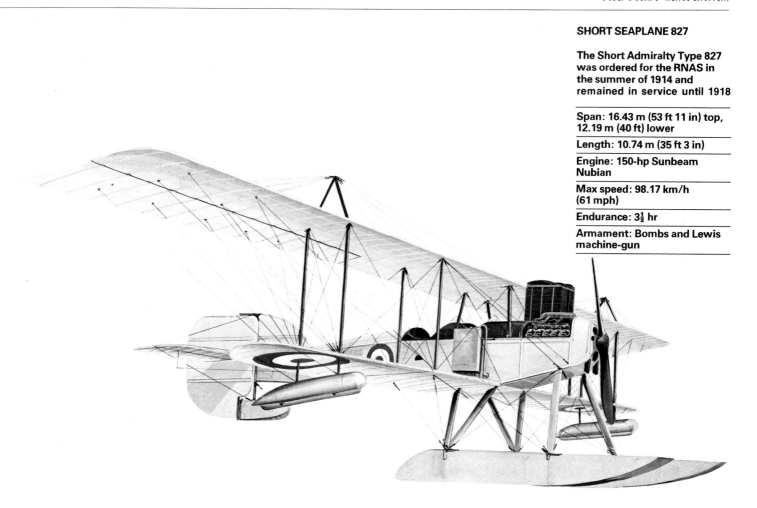

(3000 kg), in contrast with contemporary hydros which were less than half this weight at take-off. The Guidoni was probably the first twin-engine hydro. Two 200-hp, 14-cylinder Gnome rotary engines were installed in the fuselage behind the cockpit and turned coaxial propellers. The 13-ft (3.96-m) chord of the 66-ft (20.1-m) wing gave the Guidoni 800 sq ft (74 sq m) of wing area to lift its 9400 lb (4260 kg) gross weight. The Guidoni floats did not use steps in the hull design. Forlanini hydrofoils were installed to lift the floats clear of the water surface for take-off. The aircraft design, by General Alessandro Guidoni, also had a rubber suspension system for the floats to reduce the shock of take-off and landing. With all these interesting features, and the ability to carry and drop a 700-lb (318-kg) torpedo, it is surprising that this aircraft was not developed further. Instead, it was disassembled and stored at the outbreak of World War I.

The year 1913 brought additional manufacturers into the hydro arena. Burgess produced a hydro version of the Wright biplane and Frank Coffyn added a pair of multi-stepped floats to Russell Alger's Wright. Captain Hugh L Willoughby was experimenting in Florida with a hydro of original design. Burgess also tested, in January 1913, a military hydro which featured an enclosed fuselage. The wing configuration and propeller drive system were of the Wright brothers' design; Burgess was one of the licensed builders of Wright-type aircraft.

Amphibious floats were used on the Voisin 'Canard' (France), which was flown on the Seine and at Monaco, although the wheels, installed in the floats, dragged when operating in the water. Retractable wheel-floats were to be a much later development of this operationally attractive combination. The Canard configuration (stabilizer/elevator mounted on the forward fuselage) was an interest-ing aircraft design, although Voisin was not the first to use this form, nor the last: supersonic aircraft as well as small, home-built aircraft have successfully adopted the configuration in recent years.

The first 'modern' example of the single-main-float configuration was the Breguet (France), powered by the 200-hp Salmson, liquid-cooled, radial engine. The Breguet demonstrated the strong points of this float configuration by taking off from seas driven by winds of up to 60 mph (96 km/h) at Monaco in 1913 in the Schneider Race. The pilot, M Moineau, put on a spectacular demonstration, taking off and landing, apparently oblivious of the seas that grounded competing aircraft.

Caudron (France) produced an amphibious twin float-plane with the wheels drawn up into the centre of the floats. This created pockets in the floats and the obstacle of partially extended wheels caused excessive water drag similar to that experienced by Curtiss when he converted the US Navy's A-2 to the OWL in 1913. In both cases, the air resistance was reduced and take-offs from land were accomplished with no greater difficulty. Water operations were, however, a different story and tests carried out were not really satisfactory.

In 1914, floats were still designed with the scow bottom to enable the aircraft to plane quickly in spite of the low horsepower engines then available. The combination worked but the aircraft and crew took quite a beating when operating in wind and sea conditions in excess of calm. Early attempts were made to minimize these shocks by installing a shock-absorbing spring system in the float attachment struts. The 100-hp Gnome-powered Henri Farman floatplane was a Continental example of this float-and-strut combination: twin floats were attached to the hull by a spring device.

LAUNCH AND RETRIEVAL

In 1903, the Wright brothers and Dr Samuel P Langley, Secretary of the Smithsonian Institution in Washington, DC, launched a man-carrying aircraft by catapult. The Langley catapult was a spring-powered device, mounted on a houseboat. The Wrights used a gravity-powered block and tackle to launch their famous 1903 Flyer on its first successful flight.

The first take-off from a ship was from a specially constructed platform over the foredeck of USS *Birmingham* on 14 November, 1910. During 1911, Captain Washington Irving Chambers, USN, was trying to make further use of the battleship and cruiser as a platform for aircraft but it was obvious that limited deck space restricted runway availability. The deck platform was not the right solution. It clearly obstructed the operation of the ship itself, particularly of the turrets. Whatever method of launching was developed, it would have to be compact and powerful enough to launch a heavy aircraft with a very short run; it would also have to be readily positioned to enable the aircraft to be launched quickly and with the minimum interference with the operation of the ship.

Catapults are essentially single-stroke engines which develop great power. They consist of a structural steel girder having an overall length greater than the accelerated run of the aircraft being launched (approximately 60-70 feet [18-21 m]). On the upper surfaces are special rails which support a launching car which slides back and forth. The aircraft rests on the launching car to which it is secured in such a way that it will withstand the high launching forces.

Incorporated within the girder structure is a fixed cylinder in which a piston moves. The piston, through a cable, exerts force through a system of fixed and moveable sheaves, to the launching car. When the catapult is fired, whether by compressed air or gunpowder, pressure is exerted on the piston, cable, sheaves and launching car to move the aircraft at a constantly increasing speed until take-off speed is reached near the end of the run. At this time, all these parts must be decelerated rapidly through use of a hydraulic buffer which absorbs the energy of the launching car.

The first catapult tested was designed by US Navy and civilian personnel under the direction of Captain Chambers and was set up on the dock at Annapolis, Maryland, in August 1912. It consisted of a wooden carriage with rollers mounted on steel tracks. Like the Wright brothers' plane, the carriage was pulled by a cable which was attached to the crosshead of a piston working in a cylinder. The propulsion force was compressed air. The carriage and the plane were both unattached to the rails. On the first test, with a Curtiss E hydroplane (Navy A-1), piloted by Lieutenant T G Ellyson, USN, the aircraft lifted off the carriage before completing the full run and, while at a transition speed, was caught by a cross-gust of wind, which caused it to stall and dive into the water.

The catapult was removed to the Navy Yard at Washington, DC, where it was modified under the direction of Commander Holden C Richardson ('Captain Dick'), USN, Naval Constructor. Small wheels were installed to bear on the underside of the track, to hold it down, and steel straps were installed to hold the aircraft on the carriage. These

A Short seaplane Admiralty
Type 166 is hoisted out from
the seaplane carrier HMS *Ark
Royal* in January 1916. *Ark
Royal* carried five Short 166s
which were armed with three
51-kg (112-lb) bombs or a
35.6-cm (14-in) torpedo with a
Lewis gun for the observer

were automatically released at the end of the launching run.

With these modifications, the catapult was mounted on a barge at the Navy Yard and testing was resumed with Lieutenant Ellyson as pilot. On 12 November, 1912, the Curtiss E (Navy A-3) hydroplane was launched successfully from this installation.

After proving the feasibility of catapult launching, a new, more powerful design was developed at the Navy Yard. The new engine was developed to operate heavier aircraft and was then shipped to the newly commissioned Pensacola Naval Air Station in Florida, in 1914, where it was mounted on an old coal barge. The first successful flight from the catapult was made on 16 April, 1915 by Lieutenant P N L 'Pat' Bellinger, flying the Curtiss F (Navy C-2/AB-2) flying boat.

The success of this experiment led to the installation of a catapult on the USS *North Carolina*. On November 5, 1916, the same Curtiss F flying boat (Navy AB-2), flown by Lieutenant-Commander H C Mustin, made the first catapult-launched flight from a ship by flying off the stern of USS *North Carolina* in Pensacola Bay.

In 1916, catapults were installed on *Seattle* and *Huntington* to launch Curtiss R-6/R-9s which were often used at sea. They could be launched from either side of the ship.

The system had not been perfected at this date. Every launch operation resulted in the carriage dropping overboard. Even when it was retrieved, this usually resulted in damage to the carriage.

Trials were carried out by the Royal Navy, launching small, World War I, land-plane fighter-types, such as Nieuports and Sopwiths, from platforms mounted on the turrets of battleships. These installations made it possible to fly the aircraft into a quartering wind but were not completely successful. The aircraft were not always in flight when they tumbled off the end of the runway and there was no provision for economical retrieval of the aircraft and pilot after successful take-offs. A system of floats was necessary to accomplish the complete mission cycle. Flotation bags had been developed but these were an emergency measure which usually resulted in substantial damage to the aircraft and engine, the result of impact with, and submersion in, the sea. The wastage of aircraft was rather high. Similar tests were tried by the US Navy but the platforms were only as strong as the turret guns. Unfortunately the planes obscured the turret range finders and unbalanced the guns.

In 1919, Commander Kenneth Whiting, USN, suggested that a turntable-type catapult should be developed for installation on battleships and cruisers, to operate independently of the turrets. The Naval Aircraft Factory at

Far left: The Wright brothers/Langley experimental catapult-launching from a houseboat on 7 October, 1903. The catapult was a simple gravity-powered block and tackle

Left: Lieutenant T G Ellyson starts his historic catapult launch in a Curtiss E hydroplane at Annapolis, Maryland in August 1912. A gust of wind caused the aircraft to stall and ditch soon after its launch

Above: A Curtiss AB-2 clears its catapult and the carriage drops away into the water. Until buffers were fitted at the end of the catapult the carriage had to be hauled back out of the water

Below: A Curtiss A-1 at Hammondsport in position for a launch down a cable run

Right: A Curtiss A-1 on the first catapult installed at Annapolis in July 1912. The cables and compressor are visible to the left of the picture
Below left: A Curtiss AB-3 at the moment of launch from the USS *North Carolina* on 10 July, 1916. The problem with this configuration was that it obscured the main armament on the after deck
Below right: Sailors and civilian crew cluster around a Curtiss D on its ramp on the light cruiser USS *Birmingham* on 14 November, 1910. It became the first ship launched aircraft

Philadelphia was authorized to design and construct the first turntable model, which was designated Type A Mark 1. Like the first catapult at the Washington Navy Yard, this Type A was also powered by compressed air.

The Type A catapult was first tested at Philadelphia on 26 October, 1921 and was capable of launching a 3500-lb (1590-kg) aircraft at a speed of 50 mph (80 km/h) after a run of 60 ft (18 m). It was designed with a friction brake to stop the launching carriage at the end of the run.

The first ship installation of this catapult was made on the quarterdeck of USS *Maryland* in May 1922. After trials proved successful, the Naval Aircraft Factory at Philadelphia was authorized to install a catapult on the quarterdeck of each battleship and two, amidship, on each *Omaha* Class cruiser.

The Type A catapult progressed through a series of modifications. Improved controls and hydraulic brakes were developed which resulted in the redesignation of the catapults as Type A Mark 3 and Type A Mark 3, Mod 1, during the period 1922-25. Type A Mark 4 catapults were in operation at the beginning of World War II aboard *Omaha* Class cruisers.

With compressed-air catapults there was always a delay due to the requirement to recompress the air for each launch operation. In 1921, Lieutenant-Commander Hamlet of the US Coast Guard suggested the replacement of the compressed air with a gunpowder system, to expedite operation and to enable alteration to the charge to match the weight of the aircraft. To Lieutenant E F Stone of the US Coast Guard and Mr F Jeansen, Engineer in the Bureau of Ordnance, USN, goes the credit for developing the system of a gunpowder catapult. In January 1922, an experimental gunpowder catapult, which would launch a 4000-lb (1800-kg) aircraft at 50 mph (80 km/h), was developed. It was designed to be mounted on the turrets of battleships. The first test installation was on the No 3 turret of USS *Mississippi* in 1924. As before, a series of improvements and modifications resulted in changes in the designation from P-1 through P-4, Mod 1, during the period 1924-31. On the first modification, the catapult could launch a 6350-lb (1883-kg) aircraft at speeds up to 64 mph (102 km/h). The powder catapult had one great advantage. It was self-contained; it required no connection of lines or valves for its operation.

In Germany, catapults were developed by Dr Ernst Heinkel, who, because of restrictions on military aviation, adapted the catapult to commercial aviation. The Heinkel company developed catapults in 1934-36 which were mounted on German luxury passenger liners, *Bremen* and *Europa*. The purpose was to speed mail deliveries by launching small mail-carrying aircraft while the ships themselves were still several hundred miles at sea. At one stage, these catapults launched the very interesting Blohm und Voss Ha139 Nordwind, a four-engined monoplane floatplane which weighed 19 tons. At this time, the commercial possibilities were encouraging, for this was before the development of a scheduled transatlantic air service. Experience gained in these operations led to the construction of several catapult-equipped motherships from which were launched flying boats as large as the Dornier 26, normally 22 tons gross weight. In 1939, on

Below: Curtiss stands on the wing of his seaplane to attach a winch from USS *Pennsylvania*. The aircraft was lifted on board on 17 February, 1911 at San Diego and became the first to be recovered at sea
Bottom: Between the wars the Germans developed high speed mail couriers which were launched at sea. Here a Blohm und Voss Ha 139 (D-AJEY *Nordwind* North Wind) is swung aboard the MS *Friesenland* off Long Island
Right: A Curtiss SOC-3 scout-observation aircraft is recovered by a US Navy cruiser. The aircraft has taxied onto the mat and the derrick has been swung out

a test at Bremen, a 27-ton Do26 was launched from *Schwebenland*.

With the production of the Curtiss SC-1 Sea Hawk, it was necessary to increase the capacity of the catapult. The SC-1 weighed in at 9300 lb (4222 kg) gross launching weight. To accommodate the SC-1, the P-6 catapult was modified, resulting in the new designation P-6, Mod 2 and Mod 3, which could launch the aircraft at a speed of 70 mph (112 km/h).

Three additional types of catapult were developed. These were the flywheel type, designated the Type F Model 1, designed by C L Norden in 1915. The Type H and the Type C were, along with the Type F, generally for flush-deck installation aboard aircraft carriers. The XH-3, designed in 1937, was to launch flying boats and could propel a 60 000-lb (27 240-kg) aircraft at 120 mph (192 km/h).

In 1940, variations of the Curtiss SB2C Helldiver and the Grumman F4F (FM-2) were fitted with twin float gear. To launch these aircraft, the H-5 catapult was designed but never fully completed because the aircraft operation concept was dropped after a limited test programme.

The most recent catapults are the steam catapults, all based on the British designed C-11 type.

Launching seaplanes by catapult was the most spectacular aspect of the operation but the retrieval process was equally interesting.

When the sea was more than choppy, the bulk of the ship was used to smooth the water's surface. This was accomplished by the ship making a sweeping turn which effectively broke up the surface, thereby clearing and levelling

the waves and creating a landing zone. The seaplane then approached the ship upwind and landed within the cleared area. While still on the step, the seaplane was manoeuvred over a towed landing mat, where it was engaged. The landing mat, which varied in detail, according to national preference, was towed alongside or behind the base ship, usually directly under the plane-handling crane. The mat effectively broke up any surface waves, much like a sea sled. As the aircraft was run up on the landing mat, the aircraft power was cut back abruptly, causing the plane to settle and engage the float keel at the step in the retrieving feature of the mat; it thus became anchored to the mat and moved along at the same speed as the ship. Having engaged the mat by a cross-rope or a lateral batten board, a line was tossed to the crew who took the necessary action to hook the ship's crane to a lifting bridle carried in the aircraft. At this time, the aircraft was lifted out of the water and deposited on the ship's deck, usually on to a special contoured handling dolly.

The German mat component was a rubberized canvas with batten boards in lateral pockets, to hook the keel of the floats at the step. The US mat usually consisted of a rope cargo net trailed from a pole which was towed from a bridle perpendicular to the ship's keel. The rope squares effectively broke up any surface waves and also served as a link pattern to which the keel of the floats or pontoon caught. With the speed of the aircraft synchronized with the ship, the plane could then be hoisted aboard, as in the German recovery. The Japanese recovery system was most likely a variation of these systems; the only real difference was the type of mat trailed to catch the aircraft.

THE YEARS OF PROGRESS

The development of design for both seaplane floats and flying-boat hulls has been a major factor in the growing efficiency of this form of alighting gear. The development has progressed from the first planing surfaces, embodying all the hydrodynamics of a sea sled, to the highly refined hulls of the Schneider racers.

The original Fabre floats were little more than a planing surface over which was constructed a float chamber to provide buoyancy for the machine at rest on the water. The earliest forms were relatively broad-beam, shallow-chord floats. Curtiss began with this form, following Fabre, but very quickly changed to a scow configuration, of narrow beam and long chord. The smooth bottom-surface was altered slightly to incorporate longitudinal strips at the centre and at the chines. These provided a very small keel area and also served as abrasion skids, protecting the hull or float bottom when the aircraft was beached.

The next most important development was the 'step', which served to break the suction of the water. Initially these steps were very minimal breaks in the bottom surface. To improve the ability of the hull to break loose, one or more stand-pipes were installed which permitted air to be introduced into the water area immediately behind the step.

At about the same time, waterproof bulkheads were introduced to prevent the shift of bilge water when the pitch angle of the aircraft changed. Of secondary importance, these bulkheads added to the overall rigidity of the hull.

By progressive stages, the hull bottoms were developed by lowering the centre to create a keel with varying angles of flare up to the chines but they still retained a planing surface in contrast to the displacement hull of boat designs. This feature assisted in raising the aircraft out of the water to reduce drag. The designer's objective was to design a hull and airframe combination which made a smooth transition from the hydrodynamic lift of the hull to the aerodynamic lift of the supporting wing surface.

During the early stages of float design, bobtail floats were quite common. The floats used on the early Fairey FIII, which required an additional float under the rudder post to support the aircraft while at rest, were an example of this. Gradually the main floats were extended and the afterbody of the floats replaced the former appendage tail float.

Early floats were constructed of wood, with a shift to metal construction being made gradually. In the Schneider Trophy preparation in 1925, two pairs of racing floats were constructed, identical in every way, except materials. The wood floats weighed 190 lb (86.2 kg) each, the metal floats weighed 165 lb (74.8 kg) each. The wood floats failed at a pressure of 8.75 tons, the metal floats at 13.85 tons. Since those days, other materials have been used successfully. Notable among these is rubber, fibreglass and, more recently, styrofoam with fibreglass cover.

Along the way, a number of variations on the hull-step configuration were tried, including inverted Vs which made the chines the running surface rather than the keel.

With the outbreak of World War I, aircraft, like other forms of technology, took on a more menacing form. Over the land, fighters were making a name for themselves.

The hull building section of the Aviolanda factory at Papendrecht, Holland. Five Dornier Do J Wal seaplanes are under construction. Seaplane floats and hulls had to be stressed for air flight and sea landings, they were consequently very strong

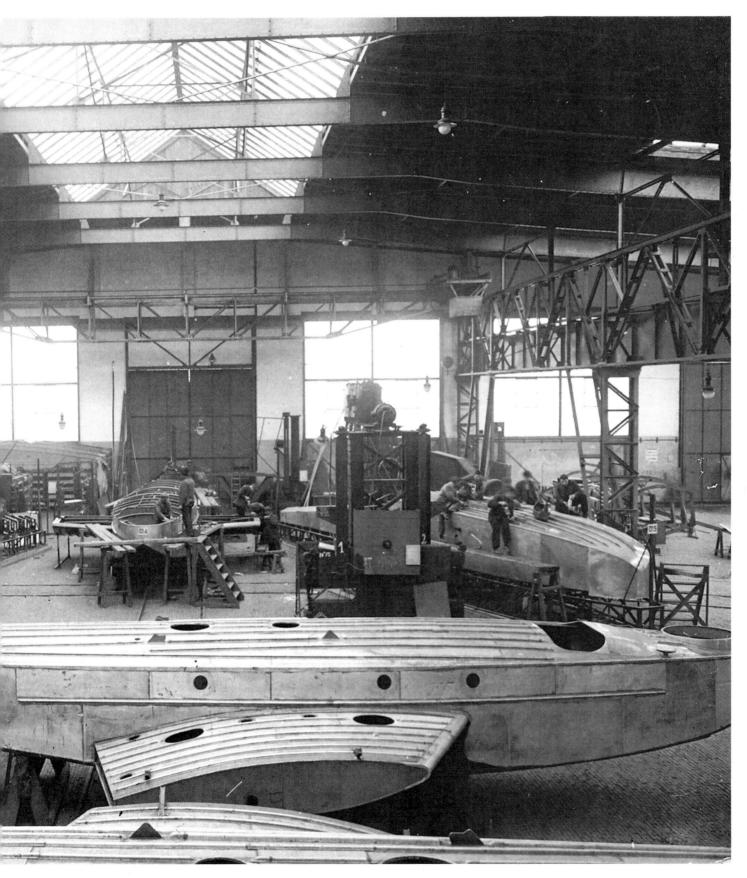

SEAPLANE HULL DESIGN

This included a step which allowed the hull to unstick on take-off. In addition a lip running round the fuselage kept the hull stable in choppy water. Enclosed cockpits protected pilots from spray on take-off. The development of floatplanes took the pilot away from the waterline, and even flying boats grew in size so that spray soaked pilots and aviators in waders became men of the past

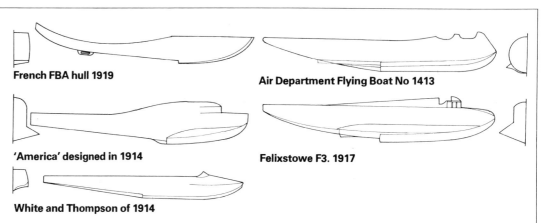

French FBA hull 1919

Air Department Flying Boat No 1413

'America' designed in 1914

Felixstowe F3. 1917

White and Thompson of 1914

SHORT SEAPLANE, TYPE 184

Known affectionately as the 'two-two-five', after its engine horsepower, the Type 184 was the first aircraft to sink a ship with a torpedo during operations off the Dardanelles

Span:	19.36 m (63 ft 6¼ in)
Length:	12.38 m (40 ft 7½ in)
Engine:	225-hp Sunbeam
Max speed:	121 km/h at 610 m (75 mph at 2000 ft)
Armament:	1 0.303-in (7.7-mm); 1 14-in (35.6-cm) torpedo or 113-kg (250-lb) bombs

Fokker, Nieuport, Spad, Sopwith and Albatros were all fighters to reckon with. On the maritime scene, the aircraft were less spectacular but more numerous in design if not in quantity.

In the early stages of the war, experimentation with waterborne aircraft increased. All the belligerents seized upon the idea of aerial observation and bombardment. The short range of the early aircraft required the construction of suitable ships to convey them to within range of action. The ungainly size and shape of the aircraft was due primarily to the low horsepower engines then available and resulted in greater wing area to compensate for this lack of power. The first folding wings were developed to reduce the dimensions for stowage aboard ships.

The earliest form of wing stowage was the panel construction of the wings of the Curtiss E hydros, which were adaptations of the Model E exhibition machines. The wing construction of these exhibition machines was considered necessary to make it possible to 'knock-down' the aircraft into convenient sizes to be crated for shipment between exhibition dates. Cross-country flights were still the

exception rather than the rule. The same idea was carried over to the navy aircraft for stowage below decks. Early in the war folding wings, which could be quickly detached and reassembled for flight, were constructed. This development allowed up to five aircraft to be stowed in the space needed for one fully-rigged aircraft.

One of the first aircraft types to use wing-folding in combat operations was the Short 184. Besides carrying out antisubmarine patrols, the 184s were embarked in seaplane carriers and participated with distinction in the Battle of Jutland on 31 May, 1916, when Flight Lieutenant F J Rutland and Assistant Paymaster G S Terwin located and reported the course and numbers of German warships to the Battlecruiser Fleet.

On the western side of the Atlantic, it was still difficult to drum up any legislative enthusiasm for the purchase of military or naval aircraft. Such activity as did exist consisted of experimental types which benefited, to a degree, by reports from the battle areas of Continental Europe. One of these experimental types, the Naval Aircraft Factory N-1, was of an unusual floatplane configuration. It

A Burgess-Dunne No 3 in service with the US Navy in 1916. Burgess had worked with the Wright brothers but joined forces with Dunne, an Englishman, in 1913. Their aircraft attracted interest with the US Army Signal Corps as well as the US Navy

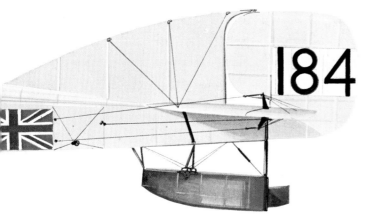

had three long floats, side by side, with the centre float larger than the two outboard floats, which were mounted directly under its twin engines. This design was attributed to Naval Constructor Holden C Richardson, US Navy. The unusual configuration of the N-1 had been tested previously on the little-known Curtiss N-6. The N-6 had impressed Richardson sufficiently for him to design the N-1 with the same float system.

At about the same time, the US Navy was testing a very unusual aircraft, the Burgess-Dunne. This was built under licence to J W Dunne of England and featured biplane wings which were swept back at about 35-40°. Aside from its unusual appearance, the machine possessed inherent stability, a rare and desirable feature in these early aircraft types.

A more conventional, though awkward-looking machine, also being tested by Burgess, was their Model HT-2 Speed Scout, which had a stilt-like appearance as it rested on its floats.

Perhaps the ultimate in complex aeronautical structures was the Gallaudet Navy Hydro, which had biplane

wings swept back at about 25°. Even less conventional was the propulsion arrangement. The cigar-shaped fuselage was separated at a point just behind the wing and a circular rotating section of the same diameter as the fuselage was installed. This section, with propeller blades protruding, rotated on a central shaft that also served to join the fore and aft sections of the fuselage to each other. The engine, which was 'buried' in the fuselage, was geared to this ring. This unusual arrangement gave pilot and observer an unobstructed view from the front of the fuselage, which was positioned about midway between the upper and lower wing panels. By comparison with the rest of the aircraft, the floats were quite ordinary. They consisted of a long central float with smaller wing-tip balancing floats.

In England, in 1917 and 1918, a number of float-types began to appear. The Wight seaplanes followed rather conventional lines, although the wing span required a veritable forest of interplane struts for strength. The Supermarine company produced an attractive pusher floatplane based on the Farman design.

At about this time the terminology of waterborne aircraft was clarified. Winston Churchill, then First Lord of the Admiralty, defined in a directive the correct designation for the flying water-craft. The term seaplane was to apply to float-equipped aircraft. The term flying boat was to apply to aircraft whose fuselage was in fact a boat-like hull. Simultaneously, there began a change in the structure of these water-craft. A gradual shift was made from the scow-type floats to the 'stepped' hulls, with varying degrees of V shape, to improve the take-off and alighting characteristics of the aircraft.

In keeping with previous products and practice, the Caproni company in Italy produced a giant triplane hydroplane, the Caproni 43, and a biplane, bimotored hydro Model 47. Conventional in general configuration, they were anything but conventional in size.

The experimental Gotha Ursinus seaplane must also be mentioned in any discussion of unconventional aircraft. Designed by the editor of the German aviation magazine, *Flugsport,* this aircraft was a classic example in support of the frequently heard arguments that editors should stick to editing and engineers to engineering. The aircraft can only be described as a flying contraption of atrocious appearance mounted on floats. Words fail to describe it. It was built by the Gotha works, which had a reputation for giant aircraft construction. With the intention of mounting the engines as close together as possible, the fuselage was mounted above the two 160-hp Mercedes engines which were mounted side by side on the lower wing with propeller arcs nearly touching. Below each engine was mounted a float, 28 ft (8.5 m) long. The combined height of the floats, the engines mounted on the lower wing, the fuselage and the upper wing all contributed to give the Ursinus a top-heavy and awkward appearance. The enclosed forward fuselage housed an observer-gunner-bombardier who enjoyed a pulpit view of a complete hemisphere forward of the biplane wings. This, in all probability, was the reason for the ugly design.

Not all floatplanes of the war years were as unconventional as the Ursinus. Gotha produced both single-engined and twin-engined floatplanes. By the end of the war, Gotha

A Dornier Rs I all-metal seaplane on its launching rails at a German naval air base in 1914. It was powered by three 240-hp Maybach engines and was a remarkably modern design for its time

alone had produced 30 different types of floatplanes. Rumpler, another well-known German company, produced floatplane variations of their own well-known, landplane observation types, as did DFW, Brandenburg and Zeppelin and other Central Powers aircraft manufacturers.

Two interesting variations, for this period of floatplane design, were the Brandenburg biplane, a German design, and the Austrian Sablatnig triplane scout. The Brandenburg floatplane of 1916 had an upper wing set close to the top of the fuselage, while the fin and rudder were disposed under the rear of the fuselage rather than above the fuselage as was customary. This same configuration was seen again in 1918 on a monoplane floatplane which, for practical purposes, used the same fuselage and tail surfaces. The purpose of this unusual configuration was to give the observer-gunner a clear field of fire to the rear, removing any possibility that the gunner, in the excitement of combat, would shoot up his own tail surfaces. Other manufacturers were not generally disposed to this concept although it showed up in 1919-30 in the United States on the Aeromarine AS ship's plane which was not produced in quantity. Manufacturers instead relied on the gunner's instinctive self-preservation motive or they added tubular arches that carried the gun barrel over or around the control surfaces and other parts of the aircraft.

Probably for different reasons than those of the US Navy, the Danish navy produced a floatplane, a flying boat and a landplane. In the USA the Naval Aircraft Factory at times designed and built aircraft on an experimental basis and in some cases produced outside designs on a limited production basis. The limited production programme was intended to monitor cost and construction details of production contracts with manufacturers. The Danish navy, on the other hand, found it impossible to attract local private contractors sufficiently skilled in aircraft production.

Spad aircraft are, of course, well known to anyone familiar with World War I, as the worthy stablemates of the Sopwith Camels and sparring partners of the equally

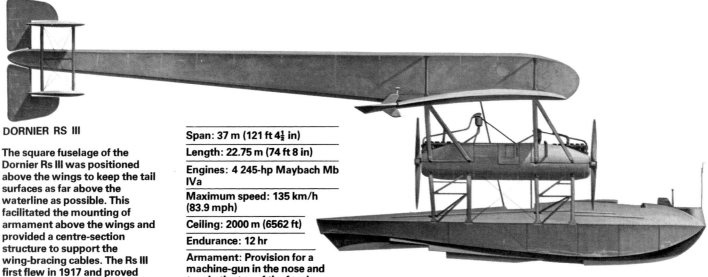

DORNIER RS III

The square fuselage of the Dornier Rs III was positioned above the wings to keep the tail surfaces as far above the waterline as possible. This facilitated the mounting of armament above the wings and provided a centre-section structure to support the wing-bracing cables. The Rs III first flew in 1917 and proved easy to fly

Span: 37 m (121 ft 4½ in)

Length: 22.75 m (74 ft 8 in)

Engines: 4 245-hp Maybach Mb IVa

Maximum speed: 135 km/h (83.9 mph)

Ceiling: 2000 m (6562 ft)

Endurance: 12 hr

Armament: Provision for a machine-gun in the nose and two in the top of the fuselage

DORNIER RS IV

Though intended as a military aircraft the Rs IV eventually came out as a civil airliner carrying 20 passengers.

Span: 37 m (121 ft 4½ in)	
Length: 22.7 m (74 ft 6 in)	
Engines: 4 245-hp Maybach Mb IVa	
Maximum speed: 138 km/h (85.7 mph)	
Ceiling: 1400 m (4593 ft)	
Endurance: 10 hr	

HANSA W12

This wooden two-seater scout fighter was in service in 1917-18

Span: 11.2 m (36 ft 9 in)

Length: 9.6 m (31 ft 6 in)

Engine: 160-hp Mercedes D3 or 150-hp Benz Bz 3

Maximum speed: 160 km/h (100 mph)

Endurance: 3½ hr

Armament: 1 or 2 fixed 7.92-mm (0.312-in) Spandau machine-guns with 1 flexible Parabellum

HANSA W29

Span: 13.5 m (44 ft 3 in)

Length: 9.36 m (30 ft 8¼ in)

Engine: 150-hp Benz Bz 3

Maximum speed: 175 km/h (109 mph)

Ceiling: 5000 m (16 400 ft)

Endurance: 4 hr

Armament: 1 fixed 7.92-mm (0.312-in) Spandau MG 08/15, flexible 7.92-mm Parabellum

famous Fokkers. Not to rest on their laurels, the Spad firm, formerly Deperdussin, brought out the high performance racing seaplane for the 1919 Schneider Cup race, and a 'Cannon Spad' for the French navy. The idea of a cannon mounted in a fighter-type was not exactly new, in the war a number of Spad XIIIs had been fitted with a 37-mm (1.46-in) cannon mounted to fire through the propeller hub. In view of the size of wooden propeller hubs, this was not too difficult to accomplish but this early postwar French navy machine mounted a 77-mm (3-in) gun synchronized to fire through the arc of the propellers, for hunting submarines in coastal waters.

Among the more ambitious seaplane designs produced by German manufacturers during the latter days of the war was a giant seaplane built by Zeppelin. This monster, designed by Dornier, was powered by four Maybach engines of 250 hp each. It had an all-metal structure with fabric wing covering. In Austria, the Sablatnig company, a newcomer to the aircraft production world, produced a biplane seaplane for the German navy and a distinctive triplane scout design which appeared at about the same time as, but was larger than, the Fokker Dr1.

The British designers had not been idle during the early stages of the war. They produced the Fairey Campania seaplane in three variations: the F16, powered by the Rolls-Royce Eagle engine; the F17 which featured a more efficient airfoil section; and the F22, which was the same aircraft fitted with the 260-hp Sunbeam engine. The name was derived from the seaplane carrier HMS *Campania*. The aircraft described were constructed to fit the stowage

capacity and hatch dimensions of this ship. Campanias were by no means small machines. Their 61 ft 7-in (18.8-m) span and 43-ft (13.1-m) length made them one of the largest types of their day.

The contemporary Westland N16 and N17 were only about half the size of the Campania types, with a span of 31 ft (9.45 m) and a length of 25 ft 3½ in (7.7 m), and incorporated a wing folding system as well. The principal difference between the N16 and N17 was the length of the floats: the N17 had longer main floats, which eliminated the need for the third float which supported the tail of the N16 when at rest on the water.

Another aircraft, the Sage 4A seaplane, powered by a Hispano-Suiza 150-hp engine, was designed for long-range patrols and was reputedly superior in performance to contemporary seaplanes and flying boats. The Fairey IIIB, designed and built late in the war, was to have a long and useful life. Variations of this design, which featured the Fairey variable camber wing (an early flap), were to see service into the late 1920s. Among other important accomplishments of the type was the first successful east-to-west crossing of the South Atlantic by Coutinho and de Cabral, of the Portuguese navy.

The Blackburn Baby was a direct descendant of the Sopwith Baby of Schneider fame. Heavy production schedules at Sopwith and urgent need for seaplanes of any design brought a contract to the Blackburn Aircraft Company to improve the performance of the Baby design until some of the experimental designs, then in the works, resulted in orders. Blackburn developed the engine

Left and below: A Curtiss N-9. The spectacular stunt flying took place in 1917 with the observer holding onto the struts above the top wing. The N-9, known affectionately as the 'sea-going Jenny' had a larger wing area than the land aircraft to support the weight of the floats

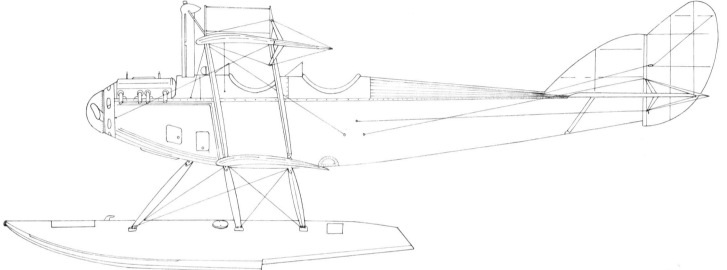

installation for the 130-hp Clerget rotary engine and the necessary drawings to enable production by a number of contractors.

The US was just beginning to catch up with its Allies in aeronautical terms, when the Armistice was declared. Among the US floatplane designs that had been approved and were in production when the war ended were the Curtiss N-9 (basically a seagoing, single-float Jenny, with greater wing area to carry the extra weight of floats) and the Curtiss R-6/9 trainer/torpedo planes fitted with two main floats. Grover Loening, a pioneer designer whose products usually were intended for water service or, at the very least, were easily converted to marine operation, produced the Loening Kitten, a diminutive shoulder-wing sporting monoplane powered with a 60-hp three-cylinder Lawrence air-cooled engine. Loening also produced a float-equipped variant of the M-8, a fighter design which featured the shoulder-wing configuration for its strut-braced monoplane wings. The M-8 was fitted experimentally with wheels which were inserted in the floats, repeating the idea tried with the Curtiss OWL.

The Fairey Pintail was an unusual compromise/combination of the designer's art. Most noticeable was the box-like fuselage of unusual depth which completely filled the gap between the two-bay biplane wings. The deep fuselage featured an unbroken line of the upper fuselage surface and only a slight upward slope to the lower fuselage terminating at the rudder post. The rudder projected below the fuselage, fairing off the appendage tail float. This of course gave the observer-gunner an unobstructed

field of fire, just as it did with the Hansa-Brandenburger. Besides these features, a retractable landing gear made this a very unusual machine, capable of a variety of duties. Modest success with the Pintail led the Fairey company to develop the concept further. The resulting Fairey Type 21 was a 1920 refinement of the Pintail concept in form and function. This was a better looking machine overall and incorporated a pair of landing wheels installed in the bottom of each float. A plane bearing a strong resemblance to the Pintail was built in Japan as the Kawanishi No 6 seaplane.

It was at this time that the name Parnall re-entered the world of aircraft production as the George G Parnall company, producing as its first design the Parnall Puffin, a seaplane amphibian which appeared to be a composite of several successful developments. The single main float had a pair of retractable wheels attached. The fuselage seemed to be suspended midway between the wing panels and the fin and rudder were attached in the ventral position, similar to the Brandenburg design of the war years. The Puffin had two more significant features – folding wings and a steerable portion of the float stern. The wing-tip floats were large by contemporary standards.

During the war, Germany had developed, besides the well-known submarine, a class of ship known as a commerce raider. This was normally a conventional merchant-man, modified to carry heavy guns. Its purpose, as in the case of the submarine, was to prey on Allied shipping. Instead of operating underwater, the commerce raider relied on surprise to accomplish its mission. To help in locating its prey, as well as for pursuit, it was decided to add a simple floatplane to the bag of tricks. One of these aircraft, built by LFG was the Putbus, a novel design lacking graceful lines but functionally designed for the job. It was a float-mounted, low-wing monoplane. The fuselage was broken at mid-point, behind the wing, for storage aboard ship. The portion from the cockpit forward appeared to be a tube of the same diameter as the Oberusel rotary engine. From the cockpit aft, the aluminium fuselage was much reduced in size, just adequate to support the empennage.

By 1920, the aircraft manufacturers who had survived the drastic cutbacks of production that followed the war years were grasping for business. To this end, some companies such as Short Brothers, developed all purpose designs, such as the Shrimp, a seaplane with a number of unusual features. The aircraft was designed for civil or military use and, within these classes, at least two engine options were offered, one low-power (160-hp Beardmore) for economy of operation in training or observation duties, and a larger 240-hp Siddeley Puma for maximum performance military use and commercial charter work. This interchangeability of powerplants was only the beginning. The Short folding-wing system permitted the operator to store the aircraft in limited hangar space. The catamaran floats were a bobtail design with a concave-hull bottom in contrast to the more conventional convex V with keel. Perhaps because of this unusual float-bottom design, shock absorbers were put in the float attachment fittings. For handling ashore, wheels could be fitted by the simple installation of a cross-axle through support tubes built into the floats; the wheels themselves were fitted to outboard extensions of the axle. All in all, this was an unusual machine prepared for use under a variety of conditions and service.

The Paul Schmitt PS 194X was a little-known, end-of-the-war French aircraft designed around the Liberty engine. It was intended for mass production but died with the Armistice, though not before successfully passing the performance tests for US Navy service. Its performance was impressive for a seaplane – 122 mph (195 km/h) and 3 hr 45-min range. It carried the pilot, plus two other crew and was armed with three machine-guns and two bomb-racks. An unusual feature was the large size of the outrigger stabilizing floats which followed the design of the Curtiss N-6 and the Naval Aircraft Factory N-1.

The German Albatros company, like Gotha and Fokker, produced a surprising number of different models. The best known, of course, were the D-3 and D-5 fighter series but the company also built seaplanes, some of which, the W4 and W8 (W for Wasserflugzüg or Water-plane), used the same wood monocoque fuselage design as the Albatros fighters. A large twin-engined pusher, twin float seaplane, the W3 was also produced and resembled the Gothas.

Famous for its giant airships, the Zeppelin airship company is less well known for machines that were heavier-than-air craft. These were produced by a separate branch known as the Freidrichshaven Flugzugbau, or FF. The designs concentrated primarily on heavy bombers but seaplanes were also much in evidence, designed for reconnaissance and torpedo launching though little is known about their operational exploits in the latter role. One of the reconnaissance types the FF33, made headlines as the Wolfchen the scout aircraft that helped the commerce raider Wolff. In a war that produced an immense number of casualties the Wolff sank a large tonnage of shipping without loss of life – a remarkable record.

Well ahead of its time in metallurgy and design was the Junkers all-metal aircraft. The first J-1, known as the Tin Donkey, was constructed primarily of thin sheet steel. With the concept proven, Junkers produced a series of machines of sheet aluminium. All these were in an era when most aircraft were still constructed of wood and fabric or, at best, steel tube, wood and fabric. The Junkers excursion into seaplane design was the Junkers C1, based on the landplane version. It was a two-place, low-wing monoplane, constructed of duraluminium, which at this early date was almost a German exclusive. The outer surface was corrugated for improved strength, a technique regarded as commonplace during the 20s but considered to be highly innovative when first introduced near the end of World War I. The floats were of catamaran configuration, not unusual in design or installation.

The name Fokker is well known as a result of the numerous aircraft supplied to the German Air Service during the war. It is also well known that Fokker was an imaginative and expansive Dutchman whose company produced a number of interesting seaplane designs following the war. Best known of these designs was the FIII-W and TII. The wing, a full cantilever wood structure, was the same construction and span (96 ft [29.3m]) as that used on the Fokker FIV transport which, known as the T-2, made the first non-stop crossing of the United States. In the TII aircraft, the wing was placed below the fuselage and the structure mounted on catamaran floats to become a torpedo plane. In the hope that the US Navy would become a customer, the Liberty engine was selected as the powerplant. Fokker's hopes for a large order did not materialize, for only one article was ordered by the US navy for test purposes. Five similar aircraft were ordered by Captain Sacadura Cabral, of the Portuguese navy.

This was a time of record setting and the round-the-world flight was attempted or planned by a number of contenders. The successful flight was made by a special US Air Services Flight. An aircraft design known as the DWC (Douglas world cruiser) was derived from the US Navy DT torpedo plane and powered by Liberty engines, the standard US powerplant left over from the war. The DWC was, like most seaplanes, adaptable to either floats or wheels. In 1924, four DWCs accomplished the feat of circumnavigating the Earth. Two of the DWCs made the complete trip and are presently exhibited in museums. The New Orleans 4 is exhibited in the US Air Force Museum at Dayton, Ohio, and the flagplane, Chicago 2, is exhibited in the US National Air and Space Museum in Washington, DC.

Another, lesser known Dutch manufacturer was producing a robust seaplane of dimensions nearly as large as the Fokker TII. This was the Van Berkel seaplane of 1922. A very rugged and simple design, it was intended for long-range reconnaissance duties in the Dutch East Indies.

The Curtiss CT torpedo plane was another specialized design of the period featuring, like the Fokker, a full

DOUGLAS DT-2

The Douglas DT-2 was modified as the DWC to become the Douglas World Cruiser during the attempt at a round-the-world flight in 1924. It had a two-man crew

Span: 15.24 m (50 ft)	
Length: 11.48 m (37 ft 8 in)	
Engine: 1 420-hp V-1650 Liberty 12A	
Maximum speed: 161 km/h (100 mph) at sea level	
Ceiling: 2134 m (7000 ft)	
Range: 441 km (274 miles)	
Armament: 1×0.30-in (7.62-mm) machine-gun	
Bombload: 1×46-cm (18-in) torpedo	

Left: A German Friedrichshafen FF33E during early air-sea rescue drills. The FF33E was normally unarmed but carried a radio for reconnaissance work. The observer has climbed down onto the float to pick up a pilot from a 'crashed' aircraft

cantilever wood wing. Unlike the Fokker, the CT did not have a fuselage in the then traditional sense. Instead, a short nacelle was installed over the centre of the deep camber wing. Outboard of this nacelle, on each side, were mounted two cowled 400-hp Curtiss CD 12 engines. Beneath the engines, two floats were strut-mounted. Structural booms, extending directly rearward from the engine nacelles and from the stern of each float, joined to support the horizontal stabilizer and elevator. Mounted on this horizontal stabilizer were two fin/rudders directly in line with the engines. The same structural design combination was to appear almost a decade later on the Italian Macchi S-55, with the floats enlarged to become twin catamaran hulls. Unfortunately, the CT, designed specifically as a torpedo carrier, was unable to lift the standard 1800-lb (817-kg) torpedo. With biplanes still in evidence with the military services of the world, the cantilever monoplane CT was a dramatic change.

The Vought UO-1 was constructed in 1923. This was a rugged service machine which marked the beginning of the air-cooled radial engine as a standard service power-plant with the US Navy. Originally, the UO-1 had been fitted with the 250-hp Aeromarine engine, but this was replaced by the 200-hp Wright Whirlwind radial. The UO-1 was to be a jack of all trades. The original order for 60 machines forecast a long life for the aircraft, since expenditure of such size was bound to ensure the use of aircraft in a variety of configurations until they were totally worn out. Such was the situation with military expenditure at this time. The UF-1, a variant of the UO-1 design, was a single-seat, float-equipped fighter with the now standard single main float and outrigger tip floats and was stressed for catapult launching from battleships and cruisers.

In 1924 the German aircraft designers were back in business. Although the terms of the Armistice prevented aircraft development in Germany, well known names such as Dornier, Udet, Heinkel and Junkers found ways to circumvent the Armistice terms by building aircraft in other countries, notably Denmark and Italy.

In the UK, as in the United States, military appropriations were being stretched to the limit. To help in the process of spreading these funds, almost all aircraft purch-

Right: A Martin T3M drops its 46-cm (18-in) torpedo during training in the late 1920s. The T3M was based on the Curtiss CS-1 torpedo-bomber which first appeared in 1923. It could carry a torpedo or bombs and was armed with a 7.62-mm (0.30-in) machine-gun in the observer's position
Below: The Martin MS-1 submarine-launched seaplane. This tiny aircraft, stowed in a hangar built into the submarine conning tower, allowed the captain to send out a spotting aircraft to locate likely targets. The concept was widely developed during the mid-1920s

ased were convertible to floats or wheels. Examples were the Parnall Plover, Blackburn Swift and de Havilland DH-9s, which had been 'remanufactured' by the aircraft development company. It was one of these reworked DH-9s that was purchased by the Norman MacMillian expedition to attempt the circumnavigation of the Earth.

A seaplane concept that kept cropping up over a period of years was the possibility of launching aircraft from submarines. The Putbus, referred to earlier, was of this design philosophy. The concept required the construction of diminutive aircraft whose structure lent itself to disassembly into units which could be accommodated in or on a submarine in a waterproof deck hangar. The aircraft had to be easily maintained and quickly assembled for operations. In the mid-20s, the Caspar U-1, a German design, fulfilled this concept.

In the US, the Martin MS-1 and the Cox-Klemin XS-1 were the best known. In Italy it was the Macchi M-53 and Piaggio P8. During World War II the idea was to surface again in the form of the Aichi Sieran, a beautifully proportioned and ingenious aircraft of much larger dimensions than its predecessors. The last known survivor of the Sieran is part of the study collection of the Smithsonian Institution's National Air and Space Museum, Washington.

One of the most highly regarded fighter aircraft in British service was the Fairey Flycatcher, often known as the 'indestructible' because of its rugged structure. The design incorporated fittings for the attachment of floats. In this form, the Flycatcher, as well as successor aircraft such as the Hawker Osprey and Nimrod, patrolled the bays and rivers of the Far East which were then under the protection of the Royal Navy. About the same time, the Fairey Type III emerged to become one of the most successful designs of this period. Intended as a long range reconnaissance machine, it was developed over a period of years, steadily improving performance. A special version, the FIII Transatlantic was fitted out to become the first to attempt the crossing of the South Atlantic in 1922. Capitan Saccadura de Cabral and Capitan Gago Coutinho of the Portuguese navy succeeded in flying from Lisbon, leaving on 30 March, 1922, to St Johns Rocks off the South American coast on the Equator. Unfortunately, a bad landing put an end to the aircraft and deprived the crew of the distinction of completing the flight as originally planned. The final stage of the flight from St Johns Rocks to Recife, Brazil was made in a standard Fairey III D of the Portuguese navy.

Other European designers were also active. The very prolific Caproni company in Italy included a number of seaplane variants in its Catalogue of large aircraft. One of these was the Ca 43. There were also small training and sporting aircraft, such as the very successful Ca 100. France and Germany were developing along traditional lines. The French produced aircraft such as the Liore and Olivier Le O H 10, a large biplane, and the Besson MB35 and MB26 seaplanes.

The MB26 was an unusual design, a sesquiplane, whose top wing was mounted directly on the top of the fuselage with the lower wing mounted between the bottom of the fuselage and the main central float. The wing-tip floats were mounted on comparatively short struts as a result of this different design. The 400-hp Lorraine-Dietrich engine gave the aircraft a speed of 102 mph (163 km/h) which was adequate for its duties as a French naval reconnaissance/observation machine. In addition to the interesting placement of structural components, the wings could be folded for storage.

Bearing a strong resemblance to the Farman Goliath, the Farman F150 Marin was a multiduty aircraft built for the French naval service. Intended to be used for torpedo carrying, bombing, photography and reconnaissance, it would have been remarkable if it succeeded in accomplishing any of these duties satisfactorily, since its powerplant consisted of two Gnome-Rhône Jupiter engines of 420 hp each. Its sheer size and all-wood construction relegated it to late World War I design and performance characteristics in an era of transition to all-metal structure. Economy of metal was its greatest attribute.

One other French seaplane deserves mention, the Villiers 10, a 1926 design for a two-seat fighter. A sesquiplane, a popular configuration in France from the days of the Nieuports of World War I, the Villiers was cleanly designed. Ailerons of narrow chord were attached to the entire trailing edge of the top wing. 'I'-type interplane struts splayed outward from the lower wing to brace the wing cellule. The fuselage, a wood monocoque structure, was of a particularly clean design. Another aircraft from Villiers, the C2F Marin, was an unusual concept. The lower surface of the fuselage had a hydrodynamic shape complete with keel. Small floats were fitted directly to the wing-tips under the interplane strut fittings. With all these features, the aircraft was a land-plane fighter prepared for forced landings in water merely by dropping its wheel landing gear. In all other respects, it was at least equal to its competitors in performance and manoeuvrability. In retrospect it may be wondered if its short life was not due to lack of confidence in the aircraft or its engines.

The German designs of this mid-20s period bore the distinctive mark of several of Germany's most prolific designers, Heinkel, Dornier and Junkers. Under several names, such as Caspar, Svenska and Heinkel, aircraft designs bearing a strong similarity began to appear. Junkers continued to produce a line of all-metal aircraft which, by design improvement stages, progressed from the F13, a single-engine plane, to the G32/24W and G31 trimotors and W33/34 single-engined designs and finally to the Ju52W, a seaplane version of the standard work-horse of the Luftwaffe in World War II. In its early development, the Ju52 was a single-engine aircraft, powered by an engine of 700-1000 hp. Two variations were powered by the Junkers L88 or BMWVII, both liquid-cooled engines, or the 700-hp Armstrong Siddeley Leopard air-cooled engine. The better known World War II version was, of course, the trimotor, the ubiquitous Ju52/3m, which was developed in 1932.

One of the largest US orders for aircraft in 1925 was the Martin SC2 torpedo/reconnaissance aircraft. As was the custom at this time, this was designed with interchangeable land/sea alighting gear. The seaplane version mounted two floats to accommodate a torpedo.

British constructors, like their US counterparts, were designing many of their aircraft as 'convertible'. Among

Below: A Vought O2U-1 floatplane from USS *Tennessee* with a Curtiss Scout from USS *Milwaukee* during a training flight in the early 1920s. The observer in the O2U appears to be an ordinary seaman up for a pleasure trip

Right: A US Navy Curtiss Hawk F6C-2 in September 1925. The pilot sits at the controls and an anonymous crewman waits ready to push the aircraft into deep water for its take-off

the more noteworthy were the Blackburn Swift torpedoplane and the Blackburn fleet spotter. The de Havilland 50a, designed for the Royal Australian Air Force in 1926, was another example designed for general utility duties. This versatile design concept was to reappear from time to time in varying sizes. Essentially, in keeping with pilot preference, the pilot sat in an open cockpit aft of the closed passenger/cargo compartment. Later, the DH Fox Moth and the Boeing Model 40 were of the same concept.

On 7 December, 1926, Group Captain R Williams, chief of the Australian air staff, began a survey flight of the mandated islands of the South Pacific in a DH50. The purpose of this survey was to acquire information on flying conditions and facilities in these territories. It was also in a DH50J that Alan Cobham (later Sir Alan) flew from London to Cape Town and back, between 16 November, 1925 and 13 March, 1926.

In 1926, the US Navy adopted the Curtiss F6C-1 and F6C-2 Hawk fighters, which were naval versions of the US Army P-1 Hawks. They were the first of the P series aircraft in US military service and, for their day, they had exceptionally good performance. The F6C-1 was powered by the well-known Curtiss D-12, a 400-hp liquid-cooled engine, and was of composite structure. It was fabric-covered and steel-tube was used for the fuselage and control surfaces. This structure was to be the basis for a whole series of aircraft. Changes in powerplants, such as the change from liquid-cooled to air-cooled engines, and

improvements in equipment with each passing year kept the basic design alive in both the US Army and US Navy service and, eventually, in the service of Turkey, Siam, China, Japan, Columbia, Cuba and several other countries.

An interesting design in the US was the Huff-Daland Pelican which was to become known for its versatility as a naval training plane. In addition to simplicity of structure and ease of maintainability, the Pelican bore more than casual resemblance to the Fokker D-VII. Examining a 'duster' version in the US National Air and Space Museum, a student of aircraft design would be immediately struck with the similarities. The thick camber wings, Fokker-style ailerons and even the tripod-style cabane struts all spell Fokker. The steel-tube structure could also be attributed to Fokker but, by this date, most, if not all, aircraft designs were basically tube and fabric. The Pelicans were rugged aircraft and were used extensively for 'aerial application'. The Pelican was the float equipped Petrel.

The Boeing company, always a strong contender in the design and production of military aircraft, produced a highly competitive design to challenge the Curtiss Hawk (F6C-1). This was the FB-3, the beginning of a long line of high performance fighters for the US services. The FB-3 was a PW-9A, refitted with a more powerful liquid-cooled engine, the Packard 2A-1500, which replaced the 440-hp Curtiss D-12, also a liquid-cooled powerplant.

The Martin T3M-1 torpedo bomber was developed from the SC-1/SC-2 and featured an all-welded tubular steel

structure which contrasted with the mixed structure of its SC-1/SC-2 predecessor.

By 1927, the Vought OU-1 had been improved to warrant a change of designation to O2U-1, which was also the beginning of the 'Corsair' designation. The name 'Corsair' was to be continued as a family name for Vought aircraft up to World War II, when it was used on the F4U inverted gull-wing fighter.

In 1927, the name 'Arado' appeared in German aircraft circles, fielding a group of interesting but simple designs. In the seaplane category, Arado built a training machine which featured twin engines of very modest power, the Siemens-Halske SH-12 air-cooled radial of 110 hp. The large, deep-cambered, cantilever monoplane wing gave it a wing loading and power loading in the same category as the de Havilland Moth and the later Piper J-3 Cub aircraft.

In the Netherlands, Fokker was back in the running with an improved design still based on the well-known Fokker concept of full-cantilever wood wings and welded-tube, fabric-covered fuselage. The Fokker TIV, which followed this basic pattern, was a twin-engine (Lorraine-Dietrich W engines of 450 hp each), high-wing, twin-float seaplane. It was constructed for the Dutch East Indies naval service for torpedo dropping and bombing duties, replacing the low wing Fokker TIII.

Along the same lines and to much the same formula, Douglas produced the Douglas T2D-1, a twin engine biplane for the US Navy. Powered by the 525-hp Wright Cyclone air-cooled engine, the T2D-1 was a torpedo bomber/observation bomber, with a span almost 30-ft (9-m) shorter than the Fokker TIV monoplane wing. Fokker was again ahead of his contemporaries with his cantilever wing design, although it was eventually to lead to his downfall as the structure was executed in wood. At this time, waterproof adhesives had not been developed and dry rot was an ever-present danger to wood. Fortunately, today, both of these problem areas have been reduced, making modern plywoods and wood structure potentially a very practical material for boats as well as aircraft.

The Blackburn aircraft company, continuing an enviable record of producing aircraft for naval operation, produced the Ripon for coastal defence and aircraft carrier use. The Ripon was a refinement of the Swift and Blackburn of an earlier era and was adaptable to floats. The change of engine from the water-cooled Napier Lion to the Bristol Pegasus resulted in a name change from Ripon to Baffin. Armament was minimal, with one synchronized forward-firing gun and one swivel-gun mounted in the observer's cockpit. Powerplant for the Ripon was the 570-hp Napier Lion XI, which also powered the Fairey FIII, a general purpose aircraft purchased by the RAF as well as the naval services of several other nations. Fairey continued the development of this durable type; it incorporated an interesting patented variable camber airfoil design, which, in a practical sense, was a full-span flap system. The Fairey FIII was one of the most versatile aircraft of its day,

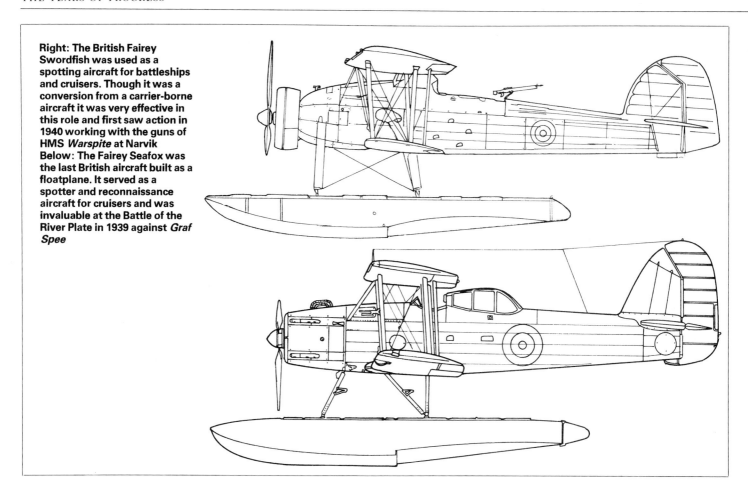

**Right: The British Fairey Swordfish was used as a spotting aircraft for battleships and cruisers. Though it was a conversion from a carrier-borne aircraft it was very effective in this role and first saw action in 1940 working with the guns of HMS *Warspite* at Narvik
Below: The Fairey Seafox was the last British aircraft built as a floatplane. It served as a spotter and reconnaissance aircraft for cruisers and was invaluable at the Battle of the River Plate in 1939 against *Graf Spee***

capable of interchanging several contemporary liquid-cooled and air-cooled engines. Also it was one of the earliest jig-built aircraft, assuring the interchangeability of components when in the field of operations.

By 1922, Heinkel was back in business as an aircraft designer but production, in keeping with the Versailles Treaty, was carried out under a contractual arrangement with Svenska AB of Stockholm. Dr Ernest Heinkel had a strong interest in float aircraft as early as World War I when he was chief designer for the Hansa Brandenburg company. Later designs were so similar that it was easy to see his progression whether in the monoplane series designated as the HE for Heinkel Einendecker or HD for Heinkel Doppledecker. Further testimony to Heinkel's pre-occupation with water-craft was the development of a series of aircraft launching catapults by the Heinkel company.

In 1928, the Martin T4M-1 replaced the T3M-2 in the US Navy service and on 1 January, 1929 Martin opened a new factory at Baltimore, Maryland, which was to be their primary manufacturing site until the late 1950s. The old Martin plant at Cleveland was purchased by the Detroit aircraft company, which produced a variant of the T4M redesignated Great Lakes TG-1 and TG-2. The new Martin plant and airfield were situated on the Baltimore waterfront where it was possible to test the seaplane T4M-1.

The Westland Wapiti was one of several aircraft types euphemistically called 'general purpose' aircraft. It was indeed a general purpose machine: in addition to doing everything in the combat categories of bombing, liaison, gunnery and the rest, it was able in emergency situations to carry its own maintenance stores up to an overload of 600 lb (272 kg). Additionally, it was designed to be manufactured from metal or wood basic structure with corrugated aluminium covering the forward fuselage and fabric cover for the rear fuselage, control surfaces and wings. This versatile machine could be fitted with floats, wheels or skis and served with the RAF, the Royal Australian Air Force and the South African Air Force in large numbers.

The early 1930's brought a development of a popular series of Hawker aircraft for service use. The Hawker company produced the two-place Hart and a naval version, the Osprey, for combined land/seaplane operations. The Osprey was accompanied by the equally attractive Fury and Nimrod, both single-place fighter configurations, powered by the Rolls-Royce Kestrel engine. The naval types, Osprey and Nimrod, were equally at home on land (or carrier) and on the water during long cruises to the Middle East and Far East with the Royal Navy.

Short Brothers produced the Gurnard with the same interchangeability of landing gear. The Gurnard was designed to accommodate the water-cooled Rolls-Royce Kestrel, as well as the air-cooled radial Bristol Jupiter. In addition to the catamaran Short floats, the Gurnard was also tested on a Short patented amphibious float gear, consisting of a single main float and wing-tip floats. The retracting wheels were fitted to a cantilever cross-tube through the top of the float. Wheels were rotated about this cross-tube from the down position, forward and upward to the retracted position. Unfortunately, in either position, the wheels were very exposed to the airstream and there was no improvement in drag reduction.

Liore-et-Olivier produced two very angular twin-engine seaplane torpedo-bombers which were almost identical, the LeO-256 and LeO-257. The 256 was powered by liquid-cooled Hispano-Suiza engines and had open cockpits for pilots and gunners. In contrast, the pilot cockpit of the 257 was protected by a coupé-type enclosure and the aircraft

LATÉCOÈRE 298D	(180 mph)
Span: 15.5 m (50 ft 10¼ in)	Maximum range: 2200 km (1367 miles)
Length: 12.56 m (41 ft 2½ in)	Ceiling: 6500 m (21 325 ft)
Engine: 1 880-hp Hispano-Suiza 12Y	Armament: 3 7.5-mm (0.295-in) Darne machine-guns; 1 torpedo or bombs
Maximum speed: 289.7 km/h	

was powered by 700-hp air-cooled radial Gnome-Rhône engines. In other respects the aircraft were identical tube-and-fabric structures.

A contemporary composite construction seaplane was the Caproni III seaplane, a long-range reconnaissance monoplane. The fabric-covered wood monoplane wing was mounted on a cavernous fabric-covered steel-tube fuselage. The powerplant was an 18-cylinder, 880-hp Isotta-Fraschini W-type engine.

Two Italian aircraft designed for catapult operation were the Piaggio P-6 and P-10, both of which were single-engine, single-float biplanes. The P-10 was an attractive three-place reconnaissance machine with a very unusual seating arrangement – a gunner position located between the forward pilot's cockpit and an observer's cockpit at the rearmost fuselage position. A neatly cowled Piaggio Jupiter air-cooled radial engine of 450 hp added to the attractive lines of this seaplane.

On the other side of the world, the Aichi company of Japan was building a neat single-place biplane fighter for the Chinese navy. A compact twin-float plane of composite structure, the Aichi AB-3 was powered by a 130-hp Jimpu air-cooled radial engine. It was not destined to offer any real opposition to the Japanese forces when the Sino-Japanese War began.

Fairey began production of the Swordfish in 1935, as a three-place torpedo/reconnaissance biplane, equally at home on wheels or floats, as was the case with many of its contemporaries. A decade later the Swordfish was still in active service although heading steadily for retirement after a gallant career as a carrier-based torpedo-bomber of World War II. It was the dinosaur of the war, a biplane in a monoplane world.

In France, in 1935, Farman produced the F271, a monster twin-engine biplane torpedo/reconnaissance seaplane, featuring very square lines of fuselage, wing and empennage. In contrast, Levasseur produced an unusual three-seat reconnaissance plane, the PL200, which was quite different from its contemporaries. It was more like an updated Curtiss CT. A pod-like fuselage supported a single air-cooled 9-cylinder radial Hispano-Suiza V9 engine producing 750 hp, mounted atop a monoplane wing. The catamaran floats were extended by a gracefully designed swept-float extension to include two vertical fins and rudders topped and connected by the horizontal monoplane stabilizer-elevator. A large aircraft for its day, the PL200 was a three-place machine with a wing span of 52 ft 6 in (16 m) and a weight of 7700 lb (3500 kg). Its top speed was about 150 mph (241 km/h).

The Bellanca bomber was a typical Bellanca design with angular wing and 'lifting' angular fuselage. It was powered by two Wright R-1820-F-3 Cyclone engines developing 715 hp each. All of the production of this model were sold to Colombia. The ungainly, large monoplane seaplane also had the characteristic Bellanca lifting struts connecting the floats to the 76-ft (23-m) span monoplane wing. It could, in modern parlance, be called 'ruggedly handsome'.

A different design concept for seaplane amphibians was begun by Grover Loening with the rather unusual Spoonbill amphibian. One of the earliest versions of Loening's concept was the US Navy's OL-8 and the US Army's OA-1A. The Loenings were particularly useful in exploration. A flight of Loenings under Commander Richard E Byrd accompanied the MacMillan Expedition to Labrador in 1926 and a flight of OA-1As made the first South American Goodwill Flight in 1927. The latter flight was a very successful event which never received the accolades that were justly deserved. In the public eye, the return of the OA-1As was overshadowed by the headlines generated by Charles A Lindbergh's solo transatlantic flight. Fortunately, the Loening OA-1A San Francisco survives and is currently an exhibit at the US Air Force Museum at Dayton, Ohio.

The design concept was kept alive by a succession of Loening designs. It was continued by the Great Lakes 61 and the Grumman J2F-1 Duck which saw extensive service

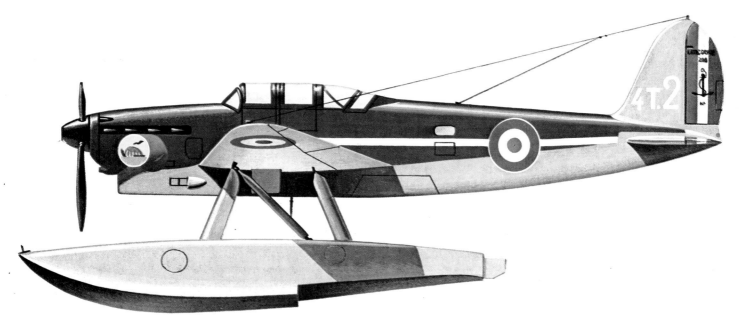

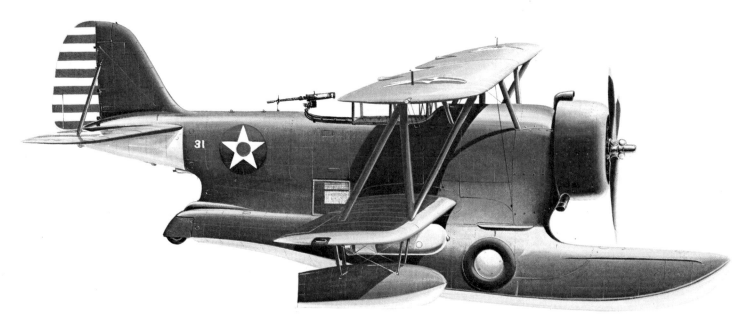

Left: A Grumman J2F-2 Duck, this was the first armed version of this amphibian, mounting two machine-guns and racks for light bombs. It was supplied to the Marine Corps in the late 1930s along with a batch to the Argentinian air force

Below: A Grover Loening OL-9 Spoonbill ferrying a US Navy Admiral in the late 1920s. The space between the float and fuselage was filled with working equipment and being faired in gave a better aerodynamic performance

in World War II as a utility aircraft with the US Navy and the US Coast Guard. The final form of the amphibian seaplane was a monoplane design, the Columbia Aircraft company XJL-1. A mid-wing design which got to the prototype stage towards the end of World War II.

French companies were producing a number of seaplanes during the mid-30s. Among those under test or construction was the Levasseur PL201, an improved version of the PL200 which crashed during tests. Liore-et-Olivier produced a three-place reconnaissance seaplane, the H-43, which was stressed for catapult launching. One design, the Loire Nieuport 200 series, was aesthetically very attractive. It was a single-engine, single-place fighter – a low-wing monoplane design with a single main float and wing-tip pontoons. An equally attractive biplane fighter, the Romano R90, was fitted with two main floats, in contrast to the Loire Nieuport. Both were powered by air-cooled radial Hispano-Suiza engines of 720 hp.

With the establishment of the Third Reich, German aircraft designers stepped up their aircraft development. Several Heinkel designs were prominent, such as the He 51 and He59. The Arado Ar95 biplane catapult floatplane was followed by the monoplane Ar196 used extensively during World War II aboard German naval ships.

In these years, Italy came forward with aircraft such as the CANT 2506B trimotor monoplane and the Caproni Ca124 reconnaissance seaplane.

The US Navy continued to develop seaplanes and still favoured the single-main-float configuration. The Curtiss SOC Seagull series, which was steadily improved during its service life, was the most numerous of the naval seaplanes of the mid-30s. A photograph of this type of aircraft on wheels shows clearly that it was designed primarily as a seaplane type, with interchangeable wheel landing gear as a poor and ugly alternative. Following the SOC-1, the succession was SOC-2, 3, 4, and SO2C, followed by the monoplane SO3C-1, 2, and 3 – all Curtiss designs. One

GRUMMAN J2F-2 DUCK

Left: This Duck is in the camouflage adopted for the Pacific in 1942. This aircraft was the last mark to be produced by Grumman

Span: 11.89 m (39 ft)	
Length: 10.36 m (34 ft)	
Engine: 1 1050-hp Wright R-1820-54 Cyclone	
Maximum speed: 283 km/h (176 mph)	
Ceiling: 8138 m (27 700 ft)	
Maximum range: 1368 km at 177 km/h (850 miles at 110 mph)	
Armament: 2 100-lb (45-kg) bombs or 2 325-lb (147-kg) depth charges	

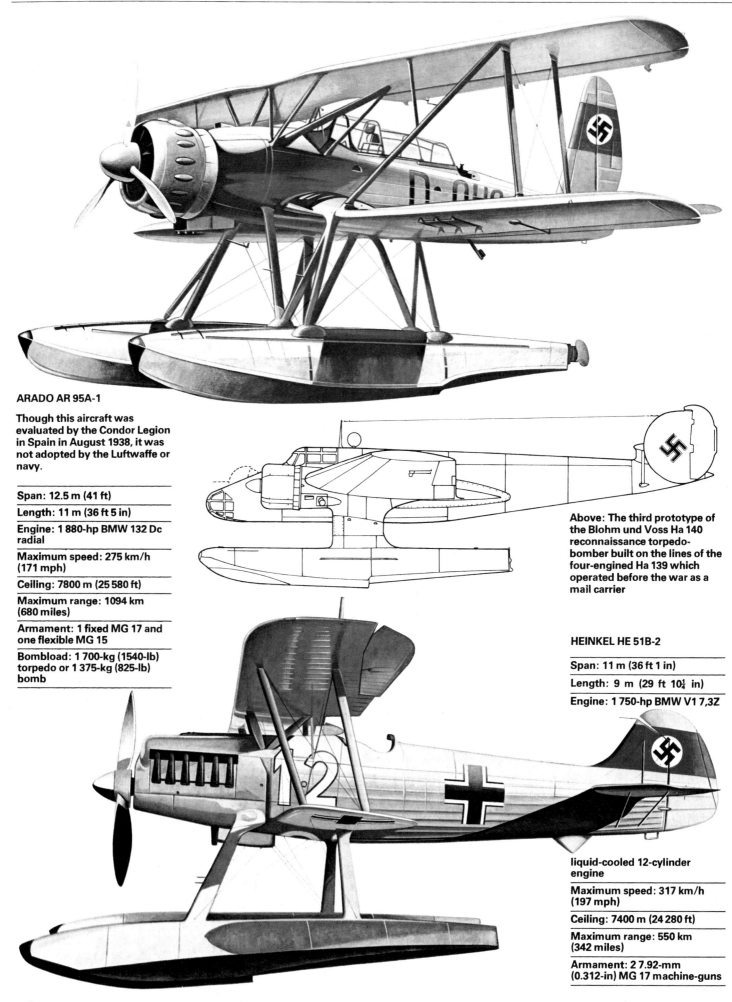

ARADO AR 95A-1

Though this aircraft was evaluated by the Condor Legion in Spain in August 1938, it was not adopted by the Luftwaffe or navy.

Span:	12.5 m (41 ft)
Length:	11 m (36 ft 5 in)
Engine:	1 880-hp BMW 132 Dc radial
Maximum speed:	275 km/h (171 mph)
Ceiling:	7800 m (25 580 ft)
Maximum range:	1094 km (680 miles)
Armament:	1 fixed MG 17 and one flexible MG 15
Bombload:	1 700-kg (1540-lb) torpedo or 1 375-kg (825-lb) bomb

Above: The third prototype of the Blohm und Voss Ha 140 reconnaissance torpedo-bomber built on the lines of the four-engined Ha 139 which operated before the war as a mail carrier

HEINKEL HE 51B-2

Span:	11 m (36 ft 1 in)
Length:	9 m (29 ft 10¼ in)
Engine:	1 750-hp BMW V1 7,3Z liquid-cooled 12-cylinder engine
Maximum speed:	317 km/h (197 mph)
Ceiling:	7400 m (24 280 ft)
Maximum range:	550 km (342 miles)
Armament:	2 7.92-mm (0.312-in) MG 17 machine-guns

other manufacturer produced a seaplane-type similar in concept to these Curtiss machines. The Vought OS2U-1 Kingfisher was highly regarded, especially by the many air crews that were rescued during World War II.

With the change-over from biplane configuration to monoplane configuration the structure also changed from composite tubular metal-and-fabric to sheet-metal. The transition was not complete, however, for fabric was still the most economical and the lightest material for covering control surfaces. This was evident in the German Arado 196A, which was produced as the primary catapult float aircraft of the German navy. Two examples of the Arado 196A exist today. One is located at NAS Willow Grove, Pennsylvania and the other is in the National Air and Space Museum collection.

The Blohm und Voss Ha140, a twin-engine reconnaissance/torpedo-bomber, owed much of its design to the four-engine Ha139 which was catapulted from a ship at sea

and arrived in New York with a load of mail.

Probably one of the most handsome floatplanes, although produced only in limited quality for the Norwegian government, was the Northrop N-3PB. This was a low-wing, cantilever monoplane. The twin floats were attached by fully cantilevered, aerodynamically clean pedestals to the wing centre section just inboard of the wing joint. The N-3PBs, intended as patrol bombers for Norwegian coastal waters, were never destined to see such service, for the outbreak of World War II and the German occupation of Norway resulted in them being used as trainers for the Norwegian air force in exile.

Another handsome aircraft, very similar in appearance to the N-3PB, was the Aichi M6A1 Sieran II, special attack aircraft. With the exception of their powerplants, the N-3PB, powered by a Wright R-1820 cyclone radial air-cooled engine producing 950 hp, and the Sieran, powered by a 1400-hp liquid-cooled Atsuta engine, were quite similar.

Right and below: The Northrop N-3PB. Despite its attractive lines this aircraft saw little service in World War II. It was operated by No 330 Squadron RAF from Iceland in an antisubmarine role in 1941-42 before being replaced by PBY-5s

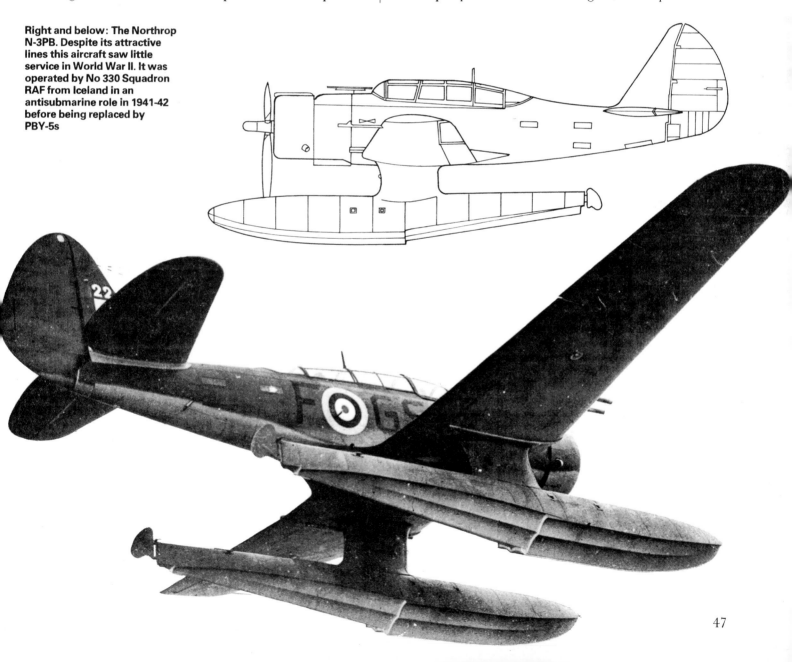

VOUGHT OS2U-3

Span: 10.94 m (35 ft 10⅞ in)

Length: 10.3 m (33 ft 10 in)

Engine: 1 450-hp Pratt & Whitney R-985-AN-2 or -8 Wasp Junior radial

Maximum speed: 264 km/h (164 mph)

Ceiling: 3962 m (13 000 ft)

Maximum range: 1859 km (1155 miles)

Armament: 1 fixed Colt Browning 0.30-in (7.62-mm) and 1 flexible machine-gun

Bombload: 2 45.36-kg (100-lb) or 2 147.4-kg (325-lb) bombs

This Aichi special attack aircraft was the last of a long series of aircraft designed for service aboard submarines. To accommodate this large aircraft, a super-submarine, the I-400, was constructed. It displaced 4500 tons and had a cruising range in excess of 41 000 nautical miles.

The Sieran could be prepared for flight in approximately one minute. This well rehearsed assembly drill required that the folded wings and tail surfaces be spread and locked in flying position. The primary mission of the Sieran and the I-400 submarine was the destruction of the Panama Canal which was scheduled for August 1945. Fortunately, hostilities ended before the attack materialized.

The final example of single-float, catapult-launched seaplanes was the Curtiss SC-1/2 Seahawk, a pugnacious-looking scout aircraft. Due to the gradual wind-down of military operations and the diminishing requirement for this category of aircraft, the SC-1/2 Seahawk saw only limited service.

The attractive but short-lived SC aircraft were cantilever low-wing all-metal monoplanes, mounted by a streamlined cantilevered pylon mount to a single central float. The clean lines were continued even to the wing-tip balancing floats and their attachment struts, which, like the main float pylon, were fully cantilevered and aerodynamically clean.

During the Pacific war, Japanese manufacturers continued to produce seaplanes, although on a limited scale. We have already mentioned the Sieran special attack plane. Others that showed refinement over the prewar technology were the Aichi E13A1 Jake and E16A1 Paul, both of which were basically twin-float low-wing reconnaissance monoplanes, and the Kawanishi E15K1 Norm 11. The latter was a beautifully proportioned two-place low-wing reconnaissance monoplane. A feature which was quite unusual on this airplane was the retraction of the outboard floats and struts into the lower wing surface. The superbly proportioned single main float was similar to the long-after-body designs later found on flying boats.

The floatplane version of the famed Mitsubishi Zero was the Nakajima A6M2-N Rufe. As attractive as the Zero from which it was derived, the Rufe was developed to provide fighter cover at distant bases before suitable landing strips were prepared. Biplane float-type observation planes were not totally absent from the Pacific war. The biplane Mitsubishi F1M2 Pete was certainly one of the most attractive floatplanes actually to see combat service. Remembering the aviation pulp magazines of the 30s, the Pete strongly resembled the attractive, imaginative and imaginary biplane fighters of the Bill Barnes fictional stories which captured the imagination of a generation of juvenile aviation enthusiasts. Graceful lines were blended into a handsome machine.

An aircraft which caused more than its fair share of attention was the Yokosuka E14Y1 Glen. This very ordinary design was also intended for submarine scouting. Its claim to fame was the widespread consternation and general nervousness created along the western coast of the United States. Shortly after the Pearl Harbor attack of 7 December, 1941, a single Glen was launched from a Japanese submarine off the coast. The single flight triggered one of the major scares of the early Pacific war period and resulted in a rash of security measures, some of which, in retrospect, can be viewed with amusement, although at the time they were introduced in all seriousness and enforced with great enthusiasm.

During the closing days of World War II a handsome scout-observation seaplane was built by the Edo aircraft company. Edo was probably responsible for the design and construction of more floats than any other single manufacturer. Their float designs ranged from the small, relatively economical designs for use with Piper Cubs to monstrous floats used on the Curtiss Condors of the Byrd Antarctic Expedition and the even larger design for use on Douglas C-47 Dakotas during World War II. Rarely did Edo go beyond the design of the floats, but in the case of the XOSE-1 they extended their talents to include the design of a complete aircraft. The result was handsome by any standard and was intended for float installation only. Its second purpose was to make use of the 12-cylinder inverted V air-cooled Ranger V-770 engine. This 550-hp engine was in production and in use in the Curtiss SO3C Seagull (Seamew) but had not been used in any other

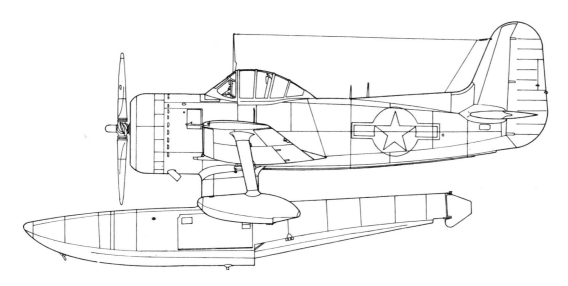

The tidy lines of the Curtiss SC-1 Seahawk which first flew in February 1944 and was in service by October that year aboard USS *Guam*. The Seahawk could carry two 113-kg (250-lb) and two 45-kg (100-lb) bombs and was armed with two 12.7-mm (0.5-in) Colt Browning machine-guns

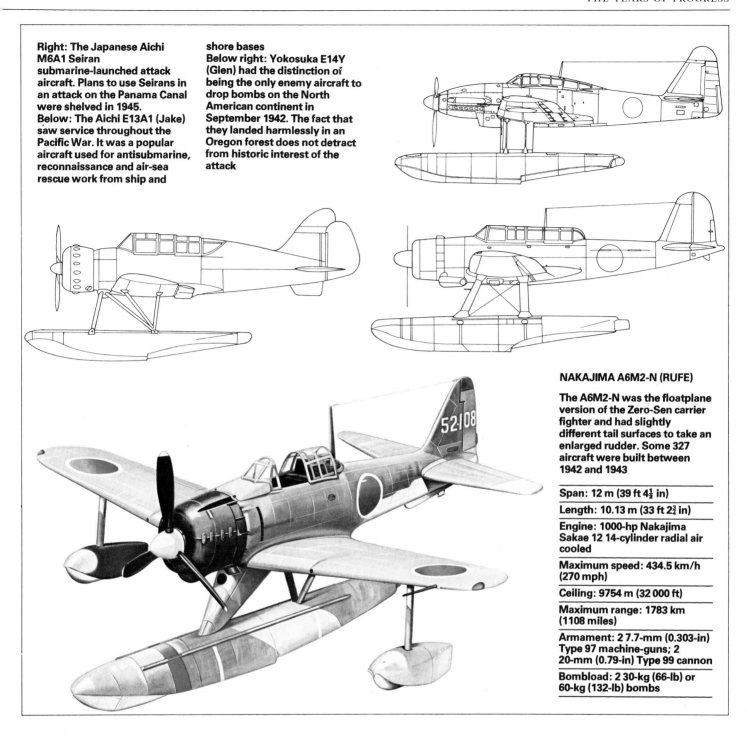

Right: The Japanese Aichi M6A1 Seiran submarine-launched attack aircraft. Plans to use Seirans in an attack on the Panama Canal were shelved in 1945.
Below: The Aichi E13A1 (Jake) saw service throughout the Pacific War. It was a popular aircraft used for antisubmarine, reconnaissance and air-sea rescue work from ship and shore bases

Below right: Yokosuka E14Y (Glen) had the distinction of being the only enemy aircraft to drop bombs on the North American continent in September 1942. The fact that they landed harmlessly in an Oregon forest does not detract from historic interest of the attack

NAKAJIMA A6M2-N (RUFE)

The A6M2-N was the floatplane version of the Zero-Sen carrier fighter and had slightly different tail surfaces to take an enlarged rudder. Some 327 aircraft were built between 1942 and 1943

Span:	12 m (39 ft 4½ in)
Length:	10.13 m (33 ft 2¾ in)
Engine:	1000-hp Nakajima Sakae 12 14-cylinder radial air cooled
Maximum speed:	434.5 km/h (270 mph)
Ceiling:	9754 m (32 000 ft)
Maximum range:	1783 km (1108 miles)
Armament:	2 7.7-mm (0.303-in) Type 97 machine-guns; 2 20-mm (0.79-in) Type 99 cannon
Bombload:	2 30-kg (66-lb) or 60-kg (132-lb) bombs

design scheduled for production. The XOSE would have made ideal use of the engine but the general wind-down of operations spelled the end of this interesting design. Only the prototype was constructed.

Since the war, it has been obvious that civil seaplanes are, as a rule, converted land-planes. Rarely are they designed for float operation and then adapted to land-plane configuration. When this sequence does occur it is usually quite apparent – the result, invariably, is an ugly duckling.

Examples of aircraft which were designed primarily as floatplanes are the Fleet Freighter (Canada), Fairchild F-11 Huskey (Canada), Fairchild Super 71 (Canada), Fairchild 82A (Canada), Noorduyn Norseman (Canada), Short Valetta (Great Britain), Short Mercury (Great Britain), Bellanca Aircruiser (US), Blohm und Voss Ha 139 (Germany) and the Fawcett F-19 (Peru).

It will be seen that many of these are of Canadian origin. In several cases, wheel landing gear was designed almost as an afterthought but necessary to bridge the period between the use of floats and skis. In Canada, this can be a very short time span but 'bush'-type flight operations must continue even during this transition period.

A special civil amphibian which, undoubtedly had military aspirations, was the Seversky SEV-3. It was a three-place low-wing all-metal monoplane equipped with twin floats which had retractable wheels built into the bottom of the floats. Operation of the landing system was rather complex. When operating from water, the wheels were retracted and the floats were locked in proper position. For runway landings the wheels were extended; this also allowed the floats to tilt freely. As the aircraft assumed a three-point position, small wheels installed in the water rudders made contact, tilting the rear of the floats upward and allowing the aircraft to complete the landing and taxiing operation on a standard tail wheel built into the fuselage tail cone.

THE SCHNEIDER RACERS

T he most important series of events in the development of floatplanes, and, in fact, of all aircraft during the 1920s, was the Schneider race series.

Through a chronological account of the contenders and winners, we can trace this development up to 1931, when the final Schneider race was flown. While the Schneider Trophy race emphasized speed, the secondary benefits were the development of testing facilities for both the aerodynamic and hydrodynamic form of the aircraft.

Technical development centred on the Schneider contestants but the effects were to ripple outwards and benefit all other hydro aircraft by the aerodynamic and structural improvements which resulted from these annual events.

The Schneider Cup, properly recorded as La Coupe D'Aviation Maritime Jacques Schneider, was to become the major incentive for the development of float-type hydroplanes. It was to be an international race, sanctioned by the Federation Aeronautique International (FAI) and open to any FAI-affiliated national aviation club. The winning club of each annual contest was to hold the trophy and be the host for the contest to be held the following year.

At the beginning of the series, adequate improvements were attainable within the time span of one year. Refinements, in the form of improved streamlining, brought forth results which enabled contestants to set new standards every year during the early years of the races. As the series progressed, it became more difficult and more costly to achieve improvements which were sufficiently advanced to win the race. In fact, races reached a stage where only major national funding commitments could make them possible. Even this recognition of the importance of the race could not overcome the problem of achieving developments within the necessary time. The development of new engineering or aerodynamic concepts to their optimum stage usually required more than a year. So hectic did these development programmes become that postponements were inevitable and contributed to the complete cancellation of the race in 1924 when only the United States' team was capable of competing. Had they flown the course the US team could have posted a second win of the trophy, having won the 1923 race at Cowes, England, with the Curtiss CR-3 flown by Lieutenant David Rittenhouse. The team could thus have placed the United States in a favourable position for retiring to their homeland with the trophy for good, since three wins were all that were necessary for a competitor to retain the trophy for ever.

The Schneider race was to become the most important of all international contests. It was to have far-reaching results for designers and companies who were active in the production of these racers through the years. The entrants in the Schneider were the pace setters in the development of floats and floatplanes.

Not all float aircraft designs followed the development lead of the Schneider winners. Floats developed for the race were designed to complement the airframes to produce a winner usually at great expense. This performance was not readily translatable into aircraft-float combinations that could earn their keep in general commercial usage when flown by pilots of average experience. In addition, the commercial floats would have had to be designed for

Lieutenant Rutledge Irvine with the US Navy Curtiss CR-3 A6081 which won the 1923 Schneider Trophy at Cowes. The 450-hp Curtiss D-12 12-cylinder V-type engine produced a maximum speed of 312 km/h (194 mph) at sea level. The Schneider Trophy was not merely a test of speed, the flying skills needed to keep the aircraft on the course and at low altitudes were considerable

The US Navy CR-3 racer which was a floatplane configuration of the Gordon Bennett Trophy and Pulitzer racers. After successes in the US the navy decided to enter the Schneider Trophy in 1923. The aircraft had already undergone alterations but as floatplanes they received wing surface radiators and enlarged vertical tail surfaces. Thus altered they took the first two places—no mean achievement for aircraft that had their airframes substantially altered in three years of harsh competitive flying

quantity production and needed to be practical to maintain in hard, everyday usage.

The first meet, held at Monaco in 1913, was only one of many meets to be held in the early formative period of aviation. In consequence, it did not create the intense interest that was characteristic of the later meets.

The French Nieuport monoplane hydro entered in the 1913 Schneider was one of the first floatplanes to use 'stepped' floats; in addition, it had interesting 'ears' added to the bow of the floats to keep the floats from 'digging in' during take-off and landing. In general terms, most floatplanes were converted land-planes. An early example of this interchangeability was the Bleriot XI. The floats and wheels were attached to the same structural members. M Garros, the noted French pilot, demonstrated the fine qualities of the Morane monoplane floatplane at the same Schneider air meet of 1913. The winner of the first meet, Maurice Prevant, was flying a Deperdussin monoplane.

The second Schneider meet was to display the most advanced aircraft available in Europe on the eve of World War I. Yet none of the aircraft entered in the 1914 Schneider were very advanced in the light of what was to come in the next four years, when the dictates of military operations led inevitably to accelerated development programmes. One possible exception was the Deperdussin, which had a clean, business-like look about it.

The 1914 meet opened with a rally planned to begin at several optional starting points and to end at Monaco. Considerable flexibility of route and departure was permitted, allowing the competitors to start any time between 1 April and 15 April. The contestants were also permitted to make a second flight to better their first attempt.

In order to equalize the distance, on arrival at Monaco, each pilot was to fly around the race course until he had completed the required 803 miles (1292 km). The mechanical problems that befell the contestants en route to Monaco emphasized the primitive state of the art. Of the original group, only five entered the Schneider.

An FBA flying boat, a production version of the Donnet-Leveque biplane flying boat, was entered by the Swiss and was piloted by Ernest Burri. All other machines entered were variations of contemporary land machines, mounted on floats. The dark-horse winner of the meet was the Sopwith Schneider Tabloid, which was flown by C Howard Pixton. This diminutive machine, powered by a 100-hp Gnome Monosoupape rotary engine, had a wing span of only 25 ft 8 in (7.8 m), and a take-off weight of only 1700 lb (772 kg).

The other entrants were, for the most part, similar to the contestants of the 1913 race: Nieuports, Deperdussins, Breguet and a pair of Morane-Saulniers. The Aviatic Arrow, the German entrant, was one of the proponents of the single-main-float configuration.

World War I required the cancellation of the race series for the years 1915-18. However, during this period, advancement in aircraft performance was accelerated and both aircraft and engine performance increased from the rather frail, low-powered kites to machines of modest power and reasonable performance.

The Sopwith Tabloid, winner of the 1914 Schneider race, found ready acceptance as a combat machine at the outbreak of the war. It was embarked aboard HMS *Ark Royal* and a number of Tabloids were sold to Japan during the later days of the war.

With the end of hostilities, the Schneider Cup contest dominated the aviation world, since the daily test of aerial combat no longer existed. International competition once again took on a less menacing format.

The 1919 Schneider race marked the introduction of the air-cooled radial engine which emerged to replace the air-cooled rotary engines of the war period. Improved design of engine and cowling increased the effectiveness of the engine's cooling fins. In addition, the rotary engine, well-known for its gyroscopic tendencies, had about reached its practical limits of power.

The 1919 Schneider race, which was held at Bournemouth, England, began on 10 September and resulted in a much disputed win by the Avro 539A, the reserve aircraft of the British team. In the 1920 and 1921 Schneider races, seaplanes were barely in the running as flying boats dominated the races.

The 1920 race at Venice proved little, competitively, for the Italian Savoia S12 flying boat, piloted by Tenente Luigi Bologna, won the race by a flyover of the course at slightly more than 107 mph (172 km/h). The 1921 race, again at Venice, was no great improvement for floatplane development, for it was a flying-boat race. The single floatplane to enter this race was the well streamlined French entry, the Nieuport-Delage, a shoulder-wing monoplane whose design was marred only by the Lamblis radiators hung on the fuselage between the float struts. Unfortunately, it was damaged in a hard landing on smooth water, which buckled the float braces and rendered it unserviceable for the race. This left the race entirely to the Italian flying boats, who set a record win with a Macchi M7, flown by Giovanni de Briganti.

In 1921 the US Services had entered air racing as a means of developing improved technology for application to service aircraft. Following the hostilities, a budget conscious Congress begrudgingly appropriated funds for a few air frames each fiscal year but refused to appropriate funds for engine development due to the well publicized superiority and the seemingly endless stock of Liberty engines in inventory, all of which were capable of repeated overhauls for apparently years in the future. This situation resulted in practically every new aircraft design being forced to use Liberty engines. The only method for the services, as manufacturers, to break out of this problem was to enter the racing game and thereby appeal to the sporting instincts of the Finance Committee and the Congress as a whole. Under the pretext of developing aircraft for the Pulitzer, an all military race, and later the Schneider, which brought in the national pride aspect, the services were funded to develop new engines – for racing purposes – and also new airframes. A cursory examination of the racing airframes makes it evident that many of them had little to recommend them for combat use. Nevertheless, lessons learned in the design of these planes and engines were to be far-reaching.

The 1922 Schneider was once again largely a flying-boat race. The refinements incorporated in this 1922 crop of boats resulted in aircraft which were aesthetically pleasing as well as aerodynamically and hydrodynamically efficient. France entered two aircraft, the CAMS 31, a single-place design powered by a 300-hp Hispano Suiza engine driving a tractor propeller, and its stablemate, the CAMS 36, likewise a tractor design of handsome proportions. Unfortunately, neither of these aircraft entered the contest, having been withdrawn prior to the actual race. This left the British entry, the Supermarine Sea King/Sea Lion II, and the Italian SIAI S51 in competition for the single-float plane entry. The SIAI S50 crashed during tests.

The Sea Lion II was a much modified version of the Sea King, with the amphibian landing gear removed and the 300-hp Hispano-Suiza engine replaced by a 450-hp Napier Lion. The S51 should have, by all odds, been the winner for it was superior to the the two Italian Macchi entries and it was later, on 22 December, to establish a speed record for seaplanes of more than 174 mph (278 kph).

Fortunately for Henri Baird, pilot of the Sea Lion, the propeller of the S51 began to delaminate as a result of immersion during the prescribed seaworthiness test. This was to restrict the pilot to power settings which did not cause the propeller to vibrate. The result was a victory for Baird and the Sea Lion and a 1923 race-site back in Britain.

The 1923 Schneider race was at Cowes, Isle of Wight. By that year the racing fever was well established.

It was also the first year in which the high cost of the race became evident. In 1921 and 1922 Curtiss-built CR-1 and CR-2 racers had dominated the US domestic land-plane races. In 1923 the CR-3 floatplanes, derived from the CR1/2, were entered in the Schneider by the US Navy.

Added to this fleet of US racing machines was a highly modified TR-3, a redesigned TS-3, which was based on the first biplane fighter specifically designed for carrier operation. This TR-3 was intended as a practice machine for the US team and, if needed, a back-up entry in case some disaster overtook the designated racing machines. In addition to the CR-3s and the trainer TR-3, the fourth US aircraft was a Dayton-Wright (Navy-Wright) NW-2. This was a powerful machine and the one favoured to win the race. However, during the pre-race flight test, the propeller apparently became damaged, tearing the 650-hp engine to pieces and eliminating the NW-2 from the race. The NW-2 had a decided advantage over the CR-3s in the power:weight ratio. The CR-3s, whose Curtiss CD-12 engines turned up 465 hp, weighed 2747 lb (1246 kg) at take-off, while the NW-2, with a 650-hp Wright T-3 Tornado engine, weighed only 2133 lb (968 kg).

The Sopwith/Hawker Rainbow, the only other seaplane entry, seemed curiously out of date; its design lacked the refinement of both the CR-3 and the NW-2. However, it should be remembered that it was in this year that the US Navy first entered the picture as an active participant: its available resources were greater, particularly with regard to float design. The Curtiss CR-3, as noted, was an improvement over the CR-2 which had given a good account of itself in the land-plane races of the two previous years.

Also of interest in the array of entries in the 1923 Schneider was a bevy of fast flying boats from Britain and France. The Blackburn Pellet and the refurbished Supermarine Sea Lion were the British entries. The French

Top: The British Supermarine Sea Lion II, winner of the 1922 Schneider Trophy, lifts off in a flurry of spray in the early 1920s
Centre: The Sopwith Tabloid at Monaco in 1914 when it was entered for the Schneider Trophy. Flown by Howard Pixton it won easily with an average speed of 139.61 km/h (86.75 mph)
Bottom: Lieutenant David Rittenhouse brings his Curtiss CR-3 to the start line of the 1924 Schneider Trophy which he went on to win that year

entered the CAMS 36 and the CAMS 38, an improved version of the CAMS 36. In the end, only the CR-3s and the Sea Lion III, again flown by Henri Baird, actually entered the race. Not unexpectedly, the race was won by Lieutenant David Rittenhouse, USN, at a speed of more than 177 mph (285 km/h), followed by Lieutenant Irvine at a speed of more than 173 mph (278 km/h), each flying a Curtiss CR-3.

The 1924 Schneider was cancelled because the competing clubs were unable to field a team of qualified aircraft. The financial and physical strain of the contest became apparent when only the US team, composed of navy aircraft and navy pilots, were able to meet the 1924 deadline. A single year of development proved insufficient to iron out the bugs of new designs or to develop older designs to meet the known minimum requirements of the succeeding race. This year was also the second year of all-out participation by the US Navy. It pointed the way to other nations for the participation of their military services if the Schneider Cup was to continue as an international sporting event.

The race was scheduled for a site in the US, in keeping with the 1923 race results. The National Aerobatic Association announced that the race would be held at Baltimore, Maryland, during the latter part of October; the water-tightness and navigability tests were to begin on 24 October.

The British entry was to have been the Gloster II, powered by an improved version of the Napier Lion engine which now produced a respectable 585 hp. Unfortunately, on its first test flight, the machine began to porpoise during its landing run, causing the collapse of the forward float attachment struts. As it sank beneath the waves, it spelled the end of the Royal Aero Club's hopes to enter the 1924 race. The Italian Club fared still worse, for their problem was even more basic – they failed to find a suitable engine. France did not field an entry either and left the US as the only contender. The US/NAA, the host club, decided to declare the 1924 contest void, thereby allowing another 12 months to prepare for the next contest.

The 1925 Schneider re-established Britain, Italy and the United States as participants. With one exception, it was to be the last time that a private civilian organization funded aircraft and crew participating in the race.

The Italian Club entered two Macchi M33 flying boats, which were also the last flying boats to be entered. Britain entered the Supermarine S4 and Gloster IIIA, both highly refined seaplanes. The former was a beautiful mid-wing monoplane (30 ft 7½ in [9.3 m] span) and the latter an equally handsome biplane (20 ft [6.1 m] span). The United States' entries were the three Curtiss R3Cs which, with floats mounted, were designated R3C-2s. An incongruous detail of these machines was the tail skid built into the fuselage for the land-plane configuration of the same aircraft, designated R3C-1. The R3C-1s were raced in the Pulitzer race (for land-planes) less than three weeks before the Schneider Trophy, and they managed to take both first and second places.

The race on 26 October was charged with excitement as well as with disappointment, for the brilliant flying of

Lieutenant James H Doolittle, the winner, was offset by the crash of the Supermarine S4 on 23 October.

The Gloster, flown by Hubert Broad, and the Macchi, flown by Giovanni de Briganti, were also-rans, with average speeds of 199 mph (320 km/h) and 168 mph (270 km/h), compared with Doolittle's winning average speed of 232 mph (373 km/h). The two other R3C-2 entries, flown by Lieutenant Cuddihy and Lieutenant R A Oftsie, failed to complete the race due to engine failure.

The day after the race, Doolittle, flying the same R3C-2, established a straightaway speed record for seaplanes of 245.7 mph (395 km/h). This aeroplane is now restored and exhibited in the US National Air and Space Museum.

The 1926 Schneider was an all-floatplane race; it had become apparent that the flying boat, even in its most highly developed form, was clearly not a match for the contemporary floatplanes as a racing machine.

After much protest by the Royal Aero Club and the Italians over the short time interval between races, the race was scheduled for October, to be held at the Norfolk Naval Air Station. This site provided decided improvements in facilities over Baltimore, where the race had been held the previous year, since all servicing facilities at Norfolk were already in place.

The US team entries were dominated by Curtiss aircraft, mostly R3C variants based on the 1925 racers. Only one US contender was of non-Curtiss manufacture; this was the Kirkham-Williams. There was also a single F6C-1 as a reserve, a float-equipped navy version of the army P-1 Hawk. The A6979 R3C-2 that had won the 1925 race retained that designation; A7054 was refitted with a Packard V-1500 engine and redesignated R3C-3, while A6978 was refitted with a more powerful Curtiss V-1550 engine and was redesignated R3C-4.

The Italian aviation industry, under pressure from Benito Mussolini, indicated that the Aero-Club d'Italia would be a contender. Though time was short, the Macchi and Fiat companies bent every back to meet the deadline for the race. The aircraft, designed by Mario Castoldi, was the Macchi M39. Five aircraft were built, two for training and three for racing. At least one of these handsome machines survives and is exhibited in the new Italian Air Force Museum just north of Rome.

While little trouble was experienced with the airframe, the Fiat company experienced problems with the engine. The racing aircraft of the day were pushing technology to the limits, for that was the intended purpose of the race series. Both the Italian industry and the US industry were experiencing developmental problems with the engines selected for the 1926 race. In the end, the Macchi M39, flown by Mario de Bernardi, won the 1926 contest at an average speed of 246.5 mph (396.7 km/h). Italy was back in the running for the retention of the trophy and the site for the 1927 Schneider race was once again to be in Venice. This time, however, it was to be a different circuit from the last.

The one year interval ensured that no really new design could be developed by Italy and the US services had withdrawn their sponsorship of new aircraft. The British, however, having by now decided that national pride was at stake, prepared for the 1927 race in a thoroughly original manner. Previous experiences had taught them that relatively few pilots had flying experience at speeds in excess of 200 mph (322 km/h). To overcome this deficiency the RAF formed what was designated the 'High Speed Flight' to provide a pool of experienced pilots for experimental aircraft operating at steadily increasing speeds.

Out of the recriminations that followed the British 1925 failure came a series of proposals which resulted in specifications for a high speed seaplane. Three designs evolved, which, after extensive tank and tunnel testing, resulted in production orders for a total of seven aircraft –

Left: The Curtiss R3C-4 was an R3C-2 re-engined with a 700-hp Curtiss V-1550. The aircraft had to withdraw from the Trophy in 1926, but a modified R3C-2 came second

Below: The British entry for the 1927 Schneider Trophy at Venice. The Supermarine Napier S-5 during a test run – N220 flown by Flight Lieutenant Webster won the trophy that year

three aircraft each from Gloster and Supermarine and one from Short. The Gloster entry was an evolutionary step from the Gloster III, a very refined biplane designated the Gloster IV.

Supermarine and Short opted for the monoplane design configuration. At Supermarine, the team feverishly prepared a worthy successor to the S4 which had come to grief at Baltimore in 1925. Instead of the beautiful, full-cantilever wing of the S4, the S5 was to have a braced low-mounted monoplane wing. The upper and lower surfaces of the wing were almost entirely covered by copper surface radiators to dissipate the heat of the Napier Lion VII engine; these replaced the drag-producing Lamblin radiators which had been used previously and found to be unsatisfactory.

The Short Brothers' entry was the Short-Bristow Crusader, which was unusual in several respects. The engine was a Bristol Mercury I, a nine-cylinder radial air-cooled design. Streamlining this proved to be quite an undertaking before the development of the low-drag NACA cowling for radial engines. The second distinguishing design feature was the wing planform, a double ellipse shape with the trailing edge having greater curvature than the leading edge and the inboard ends appearing to join together at the fuselage centreline. This was not literally true, however, for structurally it was an all-wood, two-spar, mahogany-skinned wing covered with doped silk. After overcoming all the design, engineering and construction problems of this interesting aircraft, it is sad to report that the whole effort came to nothing. During the rigging of the Crusader at Venice, the wrong halves of two turnbuckles had been connected, thereby crossing the aileron controls. Immediately after take-off Flight Officer H M Schofield appeared to execute a half roll 15 ft (4.6 m) off the water and dived into the water at a speed of about 150 mph (240 km/h). Fortunately, the wood fuselage broke at the cockpit,

throwing Schofield clear but causing him severe bruising.

There was one US entry, a private-venture project, the Kirkham-Williams. Not prepared to let the trophy go by default, when it was within reach, Lieutenant Al Williams organized what turned out to be a co-operative project to produce an entry. The Kirkham Products Corporation, of Long Island, formed by Charlie Kirkham, who had been an engine designer with Curtiss in the early days, joined forces with Williams and two former Curtiss designers, Booth and Thurston, to produce the Mercury. Since their resources were minimal, at best, they depended heavily on the assistance of individuals and industry to donate time, money and components. Under these conditions, it was surprising that anything developed. The Kirkham-Williams, powered by a donated Packard engine, bore a strong resemblance to the earlier Curtiss racers for obvious reasons; sadly, time ran out on the race deadline and it was impossible to ship the Mercury to Venice in time for the race. An extension was requested and refused.

On their home ground, the Italian team arrived with a fleet of Macchi M52s. These were improved M39 designs featuring increased power from the Fiat AS2 and AS3 engines, reduced wing span and area, refinement of the upper fuselage lines and reduced length and volume of the floats. They also had a noticeable sweepback to the wing.

The day of the race brought high winds that forced a 24-hr delay. Eventually, the surviving machines got away at about 1430 hours on Monday 26 September. One by one the contestants dropped out of the race due to engine failure. Only two aircraft completed the course. First place went to Flight Lieutenant S N Webster, flying the Supermarine S5, powered by a 900-hp Napier Lion VIIA engine, averaging 281.66 mph (453 km/h). Flight Lieutenant O I Worsley, flying a second S5, was second.

With the end of the 1927 race it became obvious to all concerned that the development of worthwhile com-

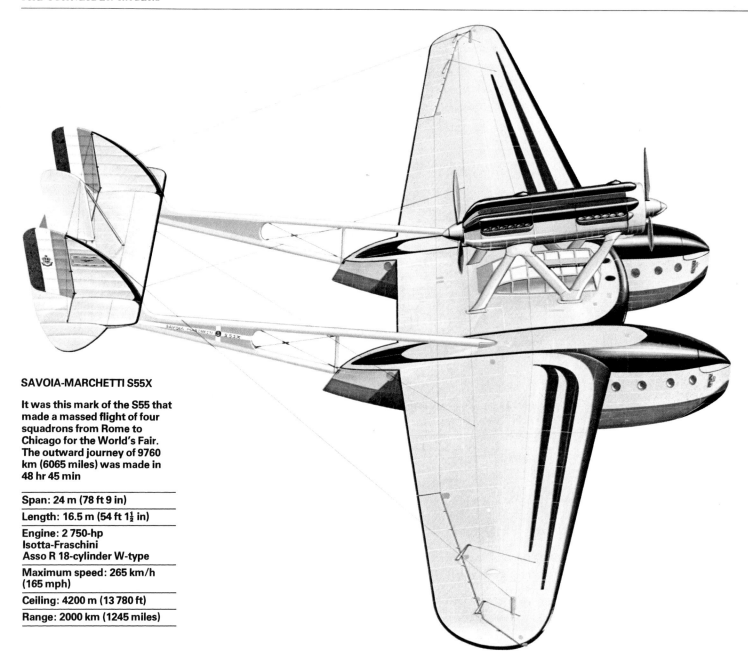

SAVOIA-MARCHETTI S55X

It was this mark of the S55 that made a massed flight of four squadrons from Rome to Chicago for the World's Fair. The outward journey of 9760 km (6065 miles) was made in 48 hr 45 min

Span: 24 m (78 ft 9 in)	
Length: 16.5 m (54 ft 1½ in)	
Engine: 2 750-hp Isotta-Fraschini Asso R 18-cylinder W-type	
Maximum speed: 265 km/h (165 mph)	
Ceiling: 4200 m (13 780 ft)	
Range: 2000 km (1245 miles)	

petitors for the race required more than the allotted 12 months. All too frequently, the contestants had merely been warmed-up developments of the previous year's machines and not really new designs. At a meeting of the FAI, held in Paris on 5 January 1928, the committee unanimously agreed to make the race a biennial meet. The multitude of technological problems, not the least of which was wing flutter, as well as the development of new metals to withstand the stresses of ever-increasing engine horsepower and the introduction of superchargers and improved fuels, all demanded more time in which to be resolved. On 29 February 1928, the Royal Aero Club announced that the next contest would be held between 29 August and 5 October 1929.

Germany and France were out of the race altogether, although France explored the possibility of entering but subsequently dropped out. This left Britain and Italy as the principal contenders. For a time it seemed that the US would also compete. The Mercury, produced by the Mercury Flying Corporation, was constructed and even shipped to England but only Britain and Italy took part. The Mercury was the product of a non-profit private group attempting to keep the US in the race. The US Navy contributed the design, models were tested at the Washing-

ton navy yard and construction was permitted at the Naval Aircraft Factory at Philadelphia. It was a development of the Kirkham-Williams racer redesigned to a mid-wing wire-braced monoplane. The resulting aircraft was underpowered for its weight, which exceeded design weight by about 400 lb (181 kg) and made it impossible to get the aircraft off the water.

In Italy there was again a singleness of purpose that had characterized the Italian efforts of 1926. Macchi, an obvious choice, Fiat, Piaggio and Savoia-Marchetti were all asked to design entrants for the race in the hope of returning the trophy to Italy.

This time Macchi produced the M67, essentially a scaled-up edition of the M52, to accommodate a more powerful engine, the 1400-hp Isotta-Fraschini. In addition to the two M67s, a single M52R was entered.

The Fiat entry was, in appearance, a small edition of the M67, except for the rather angular lines of the rudder and a high-set, horizontal stabilizer and elevator. Two very attractive and unusual machines rounded out the Italian stable of entrants, although both, as well as the Fiat, were not to fly the course. The Savoi S65 featured a two-engined configuration using the two lower powered unsupercharged engines to provide the necessary power. These

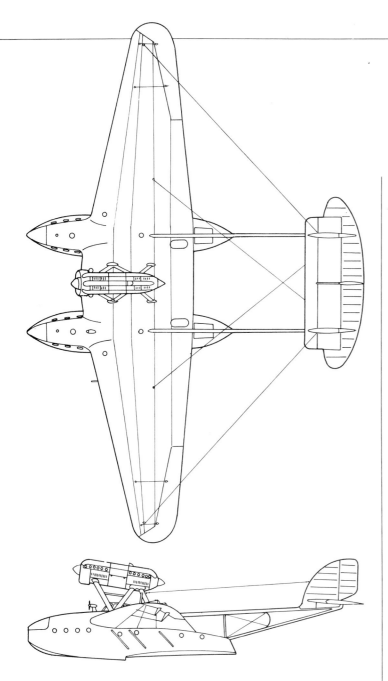

engines were mounted in a fuselage-nacelle in a pusher-tractor, push-pull installation with the pilot positioned between the engines. Two rather large floats were mounted in a fairly conventional manner, with the usual fore and aft struts wire braced to position on the outboard wing panels. Less conventional were the two boom structures attached to the rear of the floats and to the wing, over the floats. These booms extended to the rear to support the tail surfaces, the stabilizer in line with the wing and the rudder with the centreline of the fuselage.

The final and most revolutionary Italian entry was the Piaggio PC7. It was a cross between a hydrofoil boat and an aircraft. At rest on the water, the waterproof fuselage sat low, the wings resting on the water surface. Three hydrofoils were mounted beneath the fuselage, one horizontal near the marine propeller shaft and two mounted nearly perpendicular to two legs which extended downward and outward from the centreline of the hull near the centre of gravity of the hydro aircraft. It was a most unusual machine, powered by an 850-hp, 12-cylinder liquid-cooled Isotta-Fraschini engine. There were two propellers: a marine propeller was to raise the machine up onto the hydrofoils and from this position the aero propeller was to be clutched to the engine to continue the take-off and

simultaneously declutch the marine propeller. In actual practice, this proved to be too complicated. The transition from water taxi-ing to flight was never accomplished.

The British entrants' designs for the 1929 race were, for the first time, all monoplanes, although the first Gloster design proposal clung rather tenaciously to the biplane configuration. This biplane design which would have been the Gloster V, numerically, was never finalized.

The inevitable requirement for increased engine horsepower was met by the addition of a supercharger to the Napier VII engine. This increased the weight and, with the usual shifting and juggling of airframe components to restore balance, it became apparent that the upper wing would have to go. The resulting design, the Gloster VI, was a very handsome, low-wing monoplane, quite similar in appearance to, although slightly smaller than, the Supermarine entry, the S6. The wing of the Gloster was unusual for its day, although the Short Crusader of the 1927 Schneider contest and a modern turbine powered aircraft, the Republic F-91, both used a similar planform. The structure of the wing was rather conventional but the planform featured a reverse taper, the root chord shorter than the mid-plane chord and the airfoil section thicker at the mid-plane than at the root. The fuselage was a flush-riveted, semimonocoque duralanium structure.

The increased power of the Napier Lion VIIID engine required additional radiator area to dissipate the increased heat. The problem was solved, as it was with the 1925 Curtiss R3C-2, by use of the thin surface radiators which covered much of the wing surfaces.

Oil cooling, which was equally difficult, in view of the necessity to reduce drag, was accomplished by installation of a circular, flush-mounted radiator behind the cockpit. This was supplemented by surface-mounted radiators on the upper surface of the floats. Although the Gloster VI established a short-lived world speed record of 336.3 mph (541 km/h) on 12 September, 1929, technical difficulties prevented its entry in the 1929 Schneider race.

The Supermarine entry, the S6, presented its own set of problems. Increased horsepower of the new Rolls-Royce 'R' engine required increased fuselage size in which to mount the engine but the airframe was otherwise similar in appearance to the successful Supermarine S5.

In France, renewed interest in the Schneider race led to the design of four aircraft types to be entered in the 1929 race. Two of these were the Bernard HV40 and the Bernard HV42. The HV40 was fairly conventional but was grossly under-powered for the intended purpose and nowhere near the power being attained by the competitors. The Bernard HV42, on the other hand, was a very unusual configuration. It was powered by an 18-cylinder Hispano-Suiza 18R engine, developing 1680 hp at 2400 rpm at take-off. It also exceeded the much-sought-after weight-to-horsepower ratio of 1:1; the dry weight was 1144 lb (519 kg).

The thickness of the wing root of the HV42 was so deep that it appeared to be a flying wing design but the clutter of struts and wires effectively negated any real benefit from the fuselage/wing design.

Nieuport-Delage also produced two fairly conventional airframes but were still awaiting installation of the 1000-hp

Hispano-Suiza engines when, on 6 August, 1929, one of their pilots, Florentine Bonnet, was killed in a single-seat fighter aircraft while training for the race. Although it had appeared that France was once again in active competition for the Schneider trophy, the fatal accident put an end to their programme. A few days after the accident, France announced her withdrawal from the competition.

The US entry, as already stated, was the US Mercury racer, a development of the Kirkham-Williams Racer of 1927. It was a mid-wing, wire-braced monoplane design. The engine, a 24-cylinder Packard X-form engine, which had been used in the Kirkham-Williams aircraft, proved to be inadequate for this job and was replaced by an uprated Packard engine of 1500 hp. This engine, because of the race deadline, was to have been installed in the airframe while en route to England, aboard SS *Leviathan*. It was at this point that the US Navy withdrew its support and Williams was forced to back out of the race.

The race was, therefore, a contest between the Italian and British teams, reduced to the two Supermarine S6s and an S5 of the British team, and the Macchi 52R and two Macchi M67s of the Italian team. The M52R was clearly outclassed and the M67s both developed inflight problems that quickly eliminated them from the race.

The 1929 Schneider race results were: Supermarine S6 at 328.65 mph (529 km/h); Macchi M52R at 284.2 mph (457 km/h); and the Supermarine S5 at 282.11 mph (454 km/h). The British team had won, ensuring that the 1931 race would also be held in British waters.

The year 1931 was the most remembered, for it was in this year that the Schneider trophy was permanently retired. Italy were prepared to contend for the trophy. Spirits were high in Britain as a result of the 1929 win but the exchequer was low, so low in fact that, contrary to expectations, the government declared that it had no intentions of providing the funds necessary to enter the 1931 race. Their decision was most unpopular in the daily press, and in the aeronautical press particularly, for Prime Minister Ramsay MacDonald, in a moment of enthusiasm at the 1929 victory banquet, had made a public statement to the effect that 'we will win again'. As the year 1929 drew to a close, the recession was well under way and by 1930 the whole government attitude changed from its early exuberance to one of guarded fiscal policies which could not, or would not, consider such extravagances as an international air race.

Had it not been for the generosity of Lady Fanny Houston, Britain would not have entered the 1931 race, for she generously presented a cheque to the Royal Aero Club for £100 000 to underwrite the race.

The Italian team lost no time in beginning their own preparations of the aircraft on hand from 1929, the Macchi M67 and the tandem-engined Savoia S65. By the beginning of 1930, the aircraft intended for the 1931 race had been tested and tuned to the point where it was decided to attempt a world speed record with the Savoia S65. During this record attempt, on 18 January, 1930, the S65 plunged into Lake Garda, killing the pilot, Tomasso Dal Molin, who had piloted the Macchi M52R in 1929.

This left the M67 as a possible contender but in view of the 1929 experience it was decided to build a worthy

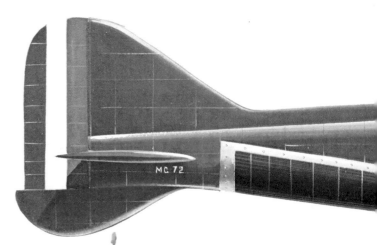

MACCHI-CASTOLDI MC72

This sleek twin engined aircraft set the world seaplane record on 23 October, 1934. It had two engines in tandem driving contra-rotating air screws

Span: 9.48 m (31 ft 1¼ in)	
Length: 8.32 m (27 ft 3½ in)	
Engine: 1 2800-hp Fiat AS6 24-cylinder V-type (2 AS5 engines in tandem)	
Maximum speed: 709.209 km/h (440.681 mph)	

successor. The Macchi-Castoldi MC72 was the result. Coming as it did from the same designer as the M67, the family relationship was not surprising. The MC72 was to be powered by an unusual powerplant, the Fiat AS6, developed from the lightweight AS5 engine. In the MC72 installation, two AS5 engines were coupled in tandem with the drive shaft of the rear engine nestled in the V between the cylinder blocks of the front engine. This rear shaft passed through the reduction gear of the front engine to

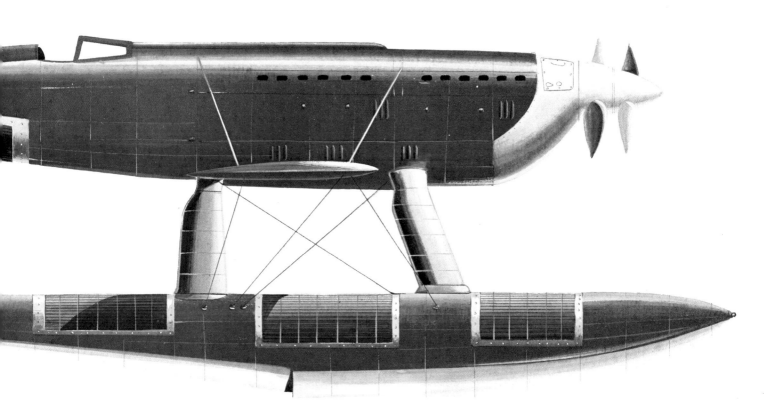

Left: A Supermarine S6 enters the water at the Supermarine Aviation Works. The S6 won the 1929 Schneider Trophy, which was held at Spithead, with a top speed of 528.88 km/h (328.63 mph). The other S6 came third with the second place going to the Italians with their Macchi M52 *bis*

Nine days before the designated date for the race, both the Italian and French Aero Clubs approached the Royal Aero Club for a postponement. Although the US team had set a precedent for such a postponement in the 1924 race, the Royal Aero Club, for reasons understood by most of the contenders, refused to postpone the 1931 race. With the government and the Air Council's decision not to provide financial support for defence of the trophy, it was most unlikely that another sponsor as generous as Lady Houston would be forthcoming should the race be postponed. It was, therefore, decided to press forward with the race and to fly the course even if other contestants were unable to be on hand to compete.

On the designated day of the contest, 13 September, 1931, only the British team was ready. The British aircraft, Supermarine S6Bs, were improved versions of the S6s of 1929 and direct descendants of the beautiful S4 of 1925.

In order to be in a position to defend the trophy, should other nations decide to enter, the British designers were hard pressed to improve on the 1929 S6. To produce an engine whose output was in excess of 2500 hp required a measure of genius from the Rolls-Royce engineers who were working on the improvement of the R engine. Engine problems were compounded by water-cooling and lubricating oil-cooling problems. Liquid temperatures soared as the engine power and rpm increased up to the level of 3200 rpm. These two problem areas were finally controlled within safe limits, for short duration race conditions. This was accomplished by increasing the area of the cooling radiators, which covered most of the surface of the wing, and the upper surface of the lengthened floats as well. The oil-cooling radiators were also expanded by using the area on both sides of the fuselage to cool the oil and for the return line on the keel of the fuselage to carry

drive one propeller; the front engine powered the second propeller independently of the first. The resulting duplex engine produced a take-off rating of 3100 hp, with a dry weight of only 2050 lb (930 kg), a 1.5 hp per pound ratio. An example of this remarkable engine is on exhibit in the Fiat Museum at Turin, Italy.

The first two MC72s experienced inflight difficulties, related to the unusual engine installations, causing crashes which destroyed the aircraft and killed their pilots.

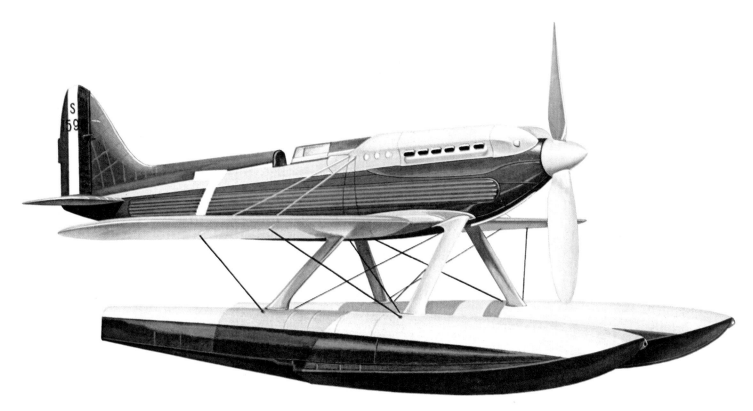

SUPERMARINE S6B

Left: The S6B, the winning aircraft in the 1931 Schneider Trophy. Flown by Flight Lieutenant J N Boothman, it reached an average speed of 547.31 km/h (340.08 mph)

Span: 9.14 m (30 ft)	
Length: 8.79 m (28 ft 10 in)	
Engine: 1 2350-hp Rolls-Royce R 12-cylinder V-type	
Maximum speed: 610.75 km/h (379.05 mph)	

Below left: Members of the 1931 Schneider Trophy team with a Supermarine S6B. The aircraft is running its engine and the team members are checking vibration
Below: S 1596 is now preserved at Southampton

the oil back to the engine for cooling and recirculation. However, the problems were not over.

The S6Bs proved incapable of getting off the water. After some experimenting with the S6As (the refined S6s of the 1929 race) the problem was discovered to be the smaller diameter propeller. When a larger diameter propeller was fitted, the S6Bs were ready for the test.

In order that there would be no mix-up resulting from the pilots competing against their team mates, a plan was devised whereby one plane would be flown around the course at a reasonable speed. In case of failure to complete the course, a back-up machine would be ready to fly the designated course. Finally, the third aircraft would be used to attempt a new record for the 2-mile (3-km) straight-away speed course.

At just two minutes past 1300 hours on 13 September, the S6B, S1595, was slipped into the water. Flight Lieutenant J N Boothman made the prescribed take-off and landing followed by a two-minute wait before taking off for

the first of seven laps to win the 1931 Schneider race and retain the trophy. His average speed for the seven laps was 340.08 mph (547 km/h). Later the same afternoon, Flight Lieutenant George Stainforth, flying S6B S1596, set a new 2-mile (3-km) speed record of 379.05 mph (610 km/h).

Two postscripts to the Schneider series are worth recording. The first was a special attempt to raise the straight-away speed record over the 400 mph (644 km/h) mark. To do this the S6B, S1595 was fitted with a special 'sprint' engine which, in addition to particular care in production, was fed a specially concocted brew which was a mixture of 60% methanol, 30% benzol and 10% acetone. On 29 September Stainforth tried to better his own record. His average speed was 408.8 mph (658 km/h).

The second post-race development involved the MC72. After ironing out numerous 'bugs' that bedevilled its Fiat AS6 engine, the Macchi MC72, flown by Francesco Agello, established a seaplane record of 440.68 mph (709 km/h), which was to stand until 1961.

PART II

SEAPLANES
AND
FLYING BOATS

A Southampton Supermarine IX takes off in a flurry of spray

THE EARLY DAYS

The art of flying off water began almost as early as flying itself. The first record of lifting off water is rightly credited to Fabre of France. However, he failed to exploit the accomplishment and it was Glen H Curtiss of Hammondsport, New York, who solved the technical details to make water flying a practical and commercially successful form of flight.

Having produced a successful hydroaeroplane, the logical next development was in the direction of what was to become the flying boat. The single-float Curtiss hydro was practical but uncomfortable. The pilot, sitting on a seat directly above the float, was exposed to the wind blast while airborne and to the water spray during take-off and landing. First a fabric spray shield was installed as on the Curtiss Navy A-2 (AH-2, OWL) with the pilot's seat positioned in its original location halfway between the float and the leading edge of the wing. Gradually the fabric gave way and was replaced by a wood structure which served the same purpose and still maintained a reasonably strong wind-resistant foredeck. As weight increased it was necessary to increase the beam of the float to provide the planing surface for quick rising out of the water and transitioning to flight.

Development of the Curtiss flying boat progressed through several stages traceable through the Curtiss aircraft designs.

The earliest version was a bat-boat configuration incorporating twin propellers. A grossly unbalanced design, in addition to the absence of a step, doomed this to failure. Undeterred, Curtiss proceeded with the design of several successors, one of which was known as a Freak Boat, all based on the flying components of the then standard Model D land-plane.

The discovery of the step to break the suction of the water and the additional wing area provided by the installation of E-type wing surfaces resulted in the first successful flying boat, sometimes referred to as the Flying Fish, in early 1912.

Development of water flying machines was underway elsewhere as well. In Britain the Sopwith Bat Boat, an amphibious aircraft, was produced in 1913. The Bat Boat hull resembled a conventional boat hull in configuration, with a sharp bow, in contrast to the Curtiss hulls of this date, which were modified scow shape with relatively flat bottoms and longitudinal rubbing strips for beaching purposes. The Bat Boat carried its tail surfaces on booms as they were on earlier machines. It was not until 1914, when Curtiss built the H-1 America, financed by Rodman Wannamaker, to compete for the Daily Mail Prize for the first transatlantic flight, that a Curtiss design showed any similarity to present-day flying boats. The America was historically the prototype for the H-4 Small America flying boats ordered by the UK during the early stages of World War I. Unfortunately, their hulls were designed for the comparative calm of Lake Keuka and were not suited for the heavy seas of the English Channel. Lieutenant J C Porte, RN, who was to have been the pilot for the transatlantic flight in the America was instrumental in purchasing the H-4s. When they arrived in England early tests convinced Porte that some drastic changes were in order. Under his direction, the hulls were redesigned and

US Navy ratings clamber over a Curtiss NC-4 to service its four Liberty 12-cylinder Vee-type engines. The flying boat completed a transatlantic crossing in 1919 from Newfoundland to Plymouth via Lisbon

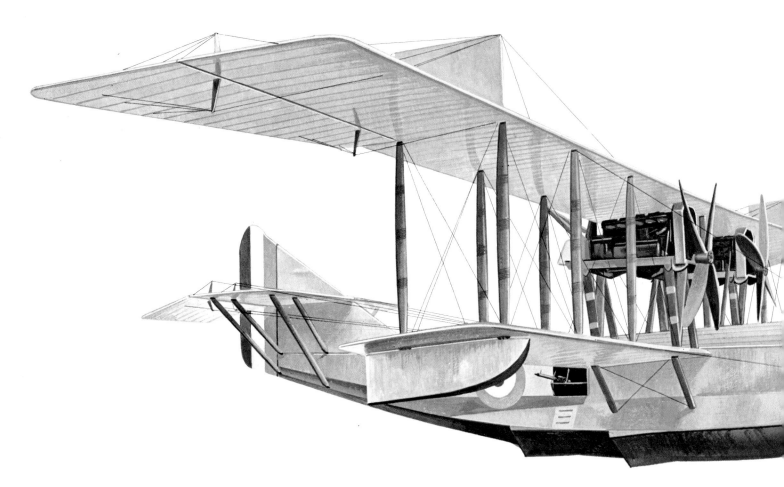

built to give them a deeper V, making them more sea-kindly when taking off or alighting, as well as structurally stronger. This development resulted in the redesignation as the Felixstowe F.1 Flying Boat. From experience gained in this redesign, Porte designed a larger flying boat, the Felixstowe F.2, named for the Royal Naval Air Station where they were designed. These were forerunners of a series of flying boats which gave excellent service through-out the war and for several years after.

In the United States, several manufacturers began devel-oping flying boats, including Burgess, a company known for boat building, and Benoist. History records that a Benoist flying boat was used to inaugurate the first regu-larly scheduled airline – the St Petersburg–Tampa Airboat Line early in 1914. Over this 22-mile (35.5-km) route, the pilot, Anthony (Tony) Jannus, carried both passengers and freight. However, the service continued for only a few weeks.

Curtiss was the most prolific of US flying boat designers, starting with the E boats, such as the USNC-1, and the numerous sporting boats. This was followed by the early F types which improved steadily in aerodynamic and hydro-dynamic detail. The Sperry F-type flying boat had a distinctive bulbous bow which housed the first autopilot. This was demonstrated in 1912 in Paris when Lawrence Sperry and his mechanic, while flying along the Seine, demonstrated the autopilot by the mechanic climbing out on the starboard wing while Sperry stood up in the cockpit,

holding his arms above his head. This was a daring demonstration for that day. If that were not enough, Sperry also developed a retractable landing gear which made beaching quite a simple task rather than the usual struggle of getting the hull properly positioned on a beaching gear to permit handling on a beach or slipway without damaging the hull.

During World War I a number of successful flying boats evolved to fill the combat requirements. The pattern of the H-4 metamorphis into the F.1 was repeated with the Curtiss H-12. During testing, it was quickly discovered that a hull which was quite adequate for lake waters of the Great Lakes of North America was inadequate for the turbulent conditions of the English Channel and the North Sea. Again, Commander Porte redesigned the hull. The resulting Felixstowe F.2 proved to be entirely successful and resulted in series production as the improved F.2A type which served well during the last years of the war. The 92-ft (28-m) wing of the H-12 resulted in its designation as the Large America to distinguish it from the H-4 which was now designated the Small America. The H-12 was aesthetic-ally more attractive than the F.2A which had a slab-sided hull, but was underpowered and had a structural weakness of the hull at the step which gave Porte reason to design a new hull using the wings and tail surfaces of the H-12. The Felixstowe boats evolved from the F.2 to the F.3, a similar but larger machine which, because of its slower speed, and greater cruising range, was better suited to patrolling the

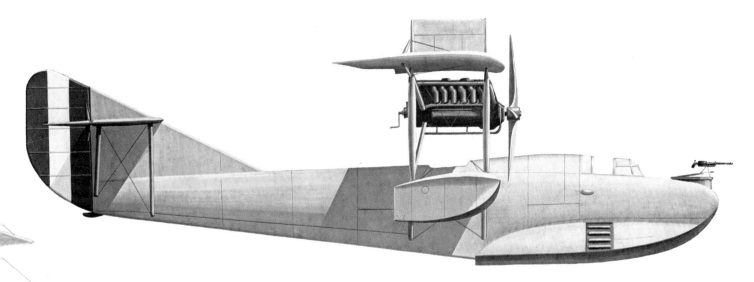

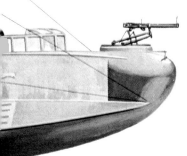

FELIXSTOWE F.2A

Named after the Royal Naval Station where they evolved, the Felixstowe series used improved adaptations of American airframes.

Span: 29.15 m (95 ft 7½ in)

Length: 14.10 m (46 ft 3 in)

Engine: 2 345 hp Rolls-Royce Eagle VIII

Max speed: 153.7 km/h (95 mph)

Endurance: 6 hours

Armament: 4 Lewis machine-guns and 2 104-kg (230-lb) bombs

CURTISS H.12

Span: 28.26 m (95 ft 8¼ in)

Length: 14.02 m (46 ft)

Engine: 2 330 Liberty 12-cylinder V-type

Max speed: 137 km/h (85 mph)

Endurance: 6 hours

Armament: 3 Lewis machine-guns and 2 104-kg (230-lb) bombs

western approaches than engaging in the more active air combat of the Channel area where the H-12s and F.2As distinguished themselves. In order to extend their time over the operating zone, a system of lighters was developed to carry the F.2As close to the target area by towing the lighter/aircraft combination behind a destroyer.

During 1917 the F.2As gave a good account of themselves and crews on antisubmarine patrol in the English Channel and the seas around the UK. On one occasion an F.2 attacked and destroyed a hydrogen-filled Zeppelin which was on a bombing/reconnaissance mission over England.

For their time, the F.2/F.2As were among the largest aircraft in operation. The wing span of the H-12/F.2A was 92 ft (28 m). Even the H-4/F.1 Small Americas had wing spans of 75 ft (22.9 m). Still larger, at 103-ft span, was the next flying boat developed at Felixstowe, the F.3, which was, in appearance, a scaled-up F.2. Operationally speaking, the F.3 was not as manoeuvrable as the F.2 and, in the eyes of the crews at least, less desirable. They did serve until the end of the war when a quantity of Felixstowe flying boats on order was cancelled. Others in process were reworked, converting them to the F.5s which were intended to remedy the shortcomings of the F.3s. Though sluggish when compared with the F.3s, the F.5s retained the desirable 6-hr endurance, a requisite for the extended range patrols. They also doubled the ordnance capacity of the F.2As, carrying four 230-lb (104-kg) bombs. Power-

plants consisted of two liquid-cooled Rolls-Royce Eagle VIII engines of 345 hp each. Unfortunately, production of the F.5s had just commenced when the Armistice was signed denying them any service. In the Felixstowe tradition, they were stretched F.3s with wing span of 103 ft 8 in (31.6 m).

In the United States, 19 F.5s were delivered to the US Navy by Canadian Aeroplanes Ltd; 137 were delivered by the Naval Aircraft Factory and 169 by Curtiss. These aircraft, powered by the 400-hp Liberty engine, were designated F.5L, to differentiate from the 350-hp Rolls-Royce Eagle VIII powered F.5s. Though they were too late for service use during hostilities, they lasted for years, much to the displeasure of US Navy crews who used them with the Atlantic and Pacific fleets long after they should have been replaced by newer, improved designs. During this service they were used to make a number of spectacular long-range flights which demonstrated aircraft mobility in the event of armed conflict. Its endurance of nearly 8 hr ideally suited the F.5L for these demonstrations. Speed was not its strong point however. The maximum speed was about 86 mph (138.5 km/h).

Lohner flying boats were about the same vintage as the F boats. These were designed and built by the Jakob Lohner Werke of Vienna. These single-engine biplane flying boats were comparable in size to the Curtiss Fs, but had much better performance. They were the best and most numerous of the flying boats built for the Austro-Hungarian navy

LOHNER TYPE L

One of the most widely used flying boats in the Austro-Hungarian Navy, the Type L had a crew of two.

Span:	16.2 m (53 ft 1¾ in)
Length:	10.26 m (33 ft 7 in)
Engine:	1 160 hp Austro-Daimler
Max speed:	105 km/h (65.2 mph)
Endurance:	about 4 hours
Armament:	1 Schwarzlose machine-gun and up to 200 kg (441 lb) of bombs

PEMBERTON-BILLING PB1

First exhibited at the Olympia Aero Show in March 1914, the PB1 was the first of nearly 55 designs from the fertile brain of Noel Pemberton-Billing.

Span:	9.14 m (30 ft)
Length:	8.23 m (27 ft)
Engine:	1 50 hp Gnome 7-cylinder rotary
Max speed:	80.5 km/h (50 mph)

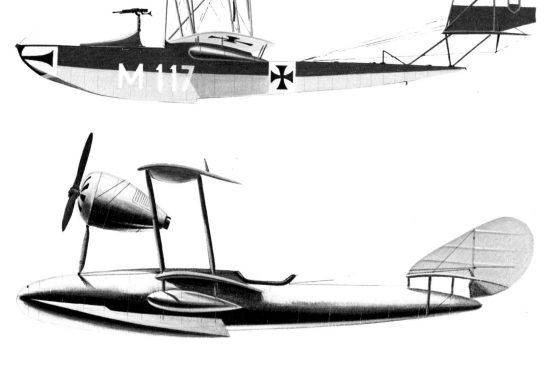

during World War I and operated in the Adriatic area against Allied shipping. They were so admired that when one was captured by the Italians during a sortie, it was copied exactly, except that the 150-hp Isotta-Fraschini engine was substituted by the Italian manufacturer for the 140-hp Hiero or the 140-180-hp Austro-Daimler engine.

Equally important in the light flying boat class during World War I was the French built FBA (Franco British Aircraft) flying boat which was the standard trainer for the French navy. A modification of the basic design was adapted for use by the British services.

A British design which was most interesting and aesthetically pleasing was the 1914 Pemberton-Billing PB1, otherwise known as the Supermarine PB1. Its 50-hp Gnome rotary engine was able to propel it through the air at 50 mph (80.5 km/h) which, in 1914, was no small task. The well-streamlined hull looked much like a cigar, probably its most outstanding feature, along with the unusual angle of its strut-mounted tractor engine. The upward angle of the thrust line was so pronounced that it appeared to be pulling the airframe up and out of the water, seemingly the first evidence of vectored thrust though it was not a variable vectored thrust as we know it today.

The Curtiss H-16, a direct development of the H-12, was a contemporary and parallel to the F.5 in development. The H-16 was a larger aircraft and an improvement over the F.5. Both benefited from experience gained in the design of the Felixstowe hulls, and saw service before the end of hostilities, but they did not have time to achieve any significant operational record.

A combined order for 75 H-16s by the British Admiralty, coupled with an order for H-16s by the US Navy, exceeded Curtiss 'production facilities' capacity, making it necessary to produce over half of the H-16s at the then new Naval Aircraft Factory at Philadelphia, Pennsylvania. Production of the H-16 continued until 1928, during which time the naval Aircraft Factory built 150 aircraft

and Curtiss produced 124. Following the war a number were sold as war surplus, some being converted to airline use for operation in the islands of the Caribbean and between the islands and Florida. One such aircraft, converted to airline fitments and painted with a gaudy fish scale design was appropriately called 'The Big Fish'. Its pilot, George A Page, was one of the early Curtiss employees who went on to become Curtiss' chief engineer and is credited with the design of the well-known C-46 Commando of World War II. The British-built H-16s were powered by the 320-hp Rolls-Royce Eagle engines and the Curtiss-built models were powered by 400-hp Liberty engines.

A flying boat of gigantic proportions was the Curtiss Model T, a monstrous triplane, with a wing span of 134 ft (40.8 m), powered by five engines. In several earlier publications this aircraft has been identified, in error, as the Wannamaker triplane. The only aircraft which can properly be called the Wannamaker was the H-1 America which, in service, was the H-4 Small America. Part of the problem of identification of the T was the secrecy surrounding its construction at Buffalo, New York. The many problems surrounding its development began with the design, started by Charles F Willard. Professor Albert F Zahm was asked to develop the powerplant system which was calculated to require 1000 hp. At the time of this design no reliable US engine combination could add up, as a practical matter, to this requirement. As a result, Rolls-Royce engines were fitted after its arrival at Felixstowe. The aircraft was so large that it could not be fully assembled at the Curtiss plant at Buffalo. The two upper wings were assembled in the workshops. The hull and two lower wings were also assembled – without the top plane. Finally, after a very secretive shipment by canal boat disguised as a load of lumber, the aircraft reached Felixstowe where it was completely assembled. A total of ten Ts were ordered, but only one was built. Only one test flight

A US Navy NC-9 flying boat, the initials stood for Navy-Curtiss who were the joint designers of this type. Work began on NC aircraft at the end of World War I

was made and, on landing, the giant model T boat was run aground on the beach, whether deliberately or by accident is not known.

Another giant aircraft was the Porte Baby, which was another experimental machine to forecast the general trend of the future of aircraft development. While the Baby did not distinguish itself militarily, it pointed the way to composite aircraft operation which was to reappear with the Short-Mayo Composite in the late 1930s. In an effort to extend the combat range of fighters, a Sopwith Pup was mounted atop the wing centre-section of the Baby. The combined power and lift of both aircraft got the composite airborne. While in flight the Pup separated from its cradle and went on unencumbered, with its fuel capacity devoted to combat requirements. In addition to the Short-Mayo Composite flying boat, the same technique was used by the USSR to lift and carry as many as five fighter aircraft to their target area where they were released for a bombing and strafing attack on a heavily fortified target. The Luftwaffe, in World War II, also used a similar technique to pair various combinations of fighters and bombers.

The last important US flying boat design of World War I was the N-C boat, for Navy-Curtiss. During the war it was proposed that the F.5Ls built in the United States be ferried to Europe to reduce the time en route and to eliminate the double handling of assembling them for test, disassembling them for shipment and finally, reassembling the planes at Felixstowe or other British bases. The proposal was not acted upon for several reasons, notably the manpower necessary to mount such a project and the marginal performance of the aircraft under these circumstances. When the NCs were designed, they were designed with this transatlantic range capability in mind. Through a long design process the balance of range, power and lifting capacity was worked into the formula to produce an aircraft with a 126-ft (38.4-m) wing span. With the end of hostilities, the US Navy was able to devote the

necessary logistic support to build and fly such a boat. It was to be powered by four Liberty engines, three tractor and one pusher. In due time the aircraft were built and the whole project was put in motion under the name of the Transatlantic Flight, which was under the command of Commander John Towers who was the US Navy's second pilot. The NCs were the last of the Big Boat designs of World War I.

After extensive preparation and the stationing of a fleet of destroyers along the route from Newfoundland to the Azores, three NCs took off on what was to be the single most significant flight in transatlantic history. While the NC-4's sister-ships, the NC-1 and NC-3, were destined not to complete the historic crossing (they had to drop out due to forced landings in the vicinity of the Azores), the NC-4 plodded along at a modest 78 mph (125.5 km/h) to become the first aircraft to bridge the unpredictable Atlantic. The crossing from Rockaway Naval Air Station, Long Island, via Trepassy, Newfoundland and the Azores to Lisbon and Plymouth, England was begun on 8 May, 1919 and completed 23 days later after an elapsed flying time of 53 hr and 58 min. It was the beginning of an era when crossing the ocean by air would surpass ships in commercial transportation of passengers and priority or high value cargo.

The NCs were different from most contemporary flying boats. Instead of an empennage attached to an extended boat hull, the tail surfaces were supported on a braced tubular wood outrigger structure similar to the earliest Curtiss D flying boat and a more contemporary Curtiss BT Flying Lifeboat developed in 1916 for the US Coast Guard. The concept of the BT was to create a seaworthy surfboat which could be flown to the scene of a shipwreck. On alighting, the wings, tail surfaces and engine could be abandoned by disconnecting a patented latch and the boat could then be operated as a conventional surfboat to rescue a ship's crew and return to shore using a secondary propulsion engine and propeller installed in the hull. The BT flew reluctantly but the disconnect feature was never developed. The NCs might have been conceived with the same idea in mind to enable the hull, on a larger scale, to survive in the event it was forced down at sea. In fact, the NC-1 and NC-3 were to determine their seaworthiness when they landed in the sea just short of their Azores destination. Both aircraft carried their crews safely on the surface of the sea until they were rescued or sailed into port. The NC-3 and crew accomplished the fantastic feat of sailing 205 miles from the point of landing into the harbour at Ponta Delgada, Azores.

Two aircraft with similar geometry, one earlier, the Sopwith Bat Boat, and one later, the Sikorsky S-38 or Navy RS-3, were amphibious but both featured a short hull and had the tail surfaces supported by booms.

With the end of the war in November 1918, thoughts turned to the normal, if slow, pattern of development in the aviation world and with it came a rebirth of the international contests to replace international combat. With a generous oversupply of military aircraft of all types, development in aviation was almost at a standstill. One of the few areas of endeavour in the world of flight was the Schneider Trophy, a race for waterborne aircraft.

THE AGE OF DEVELOPMENT

The decades from 1920 to 1940 were a period of development for flying boats and the bases from which they operated. It was also a period of exploration and improvement of the details necessary to efficiently operate them. Civil and military organizations forged ahead with design and operational improvements and the outcome of their joint efforts resulted in the development of airline and service bases in locations not previously developed for use by other aircraft. It can be shown that the building of airports in previously inaccessible locations around the world during World War II was one of the principal reasons for the transition from flying boats to land transports. The shortage of extensive airport development in most of the undeveloped nations could give reason and economic rationale to the resurrection of the flying boat today. This is particularly appropriate now, for the large fuselage cross-section which has been given as one of the technological reasons for the demise of the flying boat is no longer a factor, since the introduction of the wide-body turbojet transports.

In 1919 the Schneider race was won by a small, fast flying boat piloted by Guido Janello under very trying weather conditions. The judges, however, decreed the race results to be unofficial because of the extreme fog which caused many technical difficulties.

The following year the Schneider race was won by Italy's race team with a small flying boat design, the Savoia S-17. Again in 1921, Italy fielded a race team and this time the Macchi M-7 was the victor at 117.8 mph, putting the Italians on the verge of winning permanent possession of the trophy. (Winning the race three times in succeession retired the trophy.) This was not to be the case, for, as noted, the 1919 race results had been voided due to the irregularities caused by the fog which had invaded the course route.

It began to look as if the Italians had a complete domination of the race series with their flying boats. In 1922, the race was held at Naples with another Italian win a very real possibility. This time, however, it turned out to be a British victory won by H C Baird piloting the Supermarine Sea Lion II, at an average speed of 145.7 mph (234.5 km/h). This was the last time the race was won by a flying boat. The Sea Lion was similar in configuration to the Supermarine Ships fighter, a single-place flying boat with fighter aspirations. How effective it might have been as a fighter is somewhat in doubt, for it would appear to be incapable of the agility expected of a fighter aircraft. The competition machine, on the other hand, was the equal of contemporary aircraft, particularly those entered in the Schneider. This fortuitous win by the Sea Lion II was important to the UK from a prestige standpoint but, more important, to keep the Schneider series open and the trophy active. Unimportant as this might seem in a simple recitation of the results, it was, in fact, very important, for the designs that were to evolve from this race probably had a greater influence on the design of aircraft in general, and fighter aircraft in particular, than any other single string of events. The Schneider was the testing ground for designs which were to play an important role in World War II. Not just specific aircraft lineage was involved, for the lessons learned in the production of these racers were later

A Supermarine Napier
Southampton I refuelling in the
Bay of Naples during a flight
from Plymouth to Alexandria in
the mid-1920s. The cans of fuel
are being handed up to be
poured into the gravity feed
fuel tanks under the upper wing

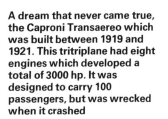

A dream that never came true, the Caproni Transaereo which was built between 1919 and 1921. This tritriplane had eight engines which developed a total of 3000 hp. It was designed to carry 100 passengers, but was wrecked when it crashed

applied to airframe details, powerplants, fuels and lubrication.

A 1921 vintage aircraft of heroic proportions was the Caproni Ca 60, a remarkable though short-lived flying boat. The triple-hydro-triplane flying boat must surely have been the wonder of its day. It is even more amazing to learn that it was designed and built as an oversized model of a type intended to be a transatlantic transport aircraft. It is not such a strange concept when one considers that the largest production bombers of World War I bore the distinguished name of Caproni. Of contemporary interest is the fact that the wing floats and the bow of this monster aircraft have been preserved in the Museo Caproni just outside Milan, Italy. When viewed in the light of today, its configuration strikes one as rather odd, consisting of triple sets of triplane wings, without empennage. The control of vertical movement of the aircraft was produced by flaps, or elevators mounted on the centre bank of triplane wings. Apparently G Caproni was not alone in wondering about multiple banks of wings, for the following year, in 1922, Max Oertz of Hamburg tested the Oertz Schooner. This was a double biplane flying boat and, if further precedent for tandem wing aircraft is necessary, one needs only to look at the Langley Aerodrome of 1903, which was a tandem monoplane. Unfortunately, all three designs were short-lived. The Caproni, powered by eight 400-hp Liberty engines, had a short but eventful operating life. It had accommodation for 100 passengers, an accomplishment worthy of note, when contemporary machines were hard pressed to carry more than 15 or 20 passengers. It did fly, however, and made its test flight, over a mile, on 2 March, 1921. A second flight on 4 March resulted in a bad landing with major damage requiring complete rebuilding if the tests were to continue. The aircraft was not rebuilt, but was disassembled. Imagine, if you will, a machine of comparable size and complexity in the present day. Even more amazing is the fact that it was operated by a single pilot, with a whole team of engineers required to control the powerplants which were linked together by a ship's type electrical signal system.

The year 1922 was when the Dornier J or Wal (Whale) made its first appearance. This was to be one of the workhorse designs of the 1920s. Its lines were teutonic and its performance, with a variety of engines, was always to be admired. The configuration of the Wal was to prove so basic that its descendant, the Dornier Do18, saw service as recently as World War II. Designed in the period of the prohibition of aircraft construction by Germany, under the terms of the Armistice, the Wal was produced under licence in Italy. It was produced in large quantities, reaching at least 300 units and was used in the services of Italy, Spain and the Netherlands, while commercial use of this type was made by Lufthansa and Aero Lloyd, Aero Espresso in Italy, Varig in Brazil, SCATADA in Columbia and Nikon Koku in Japan.

The Wal was capable of being catapult-launched from ships at sea. To develop this launching feature into a workable system, two ships were built to launch and maintain the Lufthansa Wals. These base ships, the Westfalen and Schwabenland, developed the launch and retrieval systems to a fine degree, launching more than 300

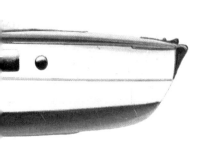

DORNIER DoJ WAL

Capable of carrying eight to ten passengers, the Wal (Whale) was initially built in Italy to avoid the restrictions imposed by the Allies after World War I

Span: 23.20 m (76 ft 1¼ in)	
Length: 18.20 m (59 ft 8¼ in)	
Engine: 2 600 hp BMW VI 12-cylinder V-types	
Max speed: 225 km/h (140 mph)	
Range: 2200 km (1365 miles)	

flights en route between South America and Africa across the South Atlantic Ocean. Numerous exploration and pioneering flights across the Atlantic and to the Arctic were made by the Wals. Captain Frank H Courtney, RFC, made two unsuccessful transatlantic attempts using a Wal, and Count Locatelli, the Italian pioneer, flew another in his transatlantic attempt in 1924, but he was forced down short of his destination. The seaworthiness of the Wal was an important factor in the rescue of Locatelli and his crew by the support ships associated with the first round-the-world flight by the US Army Service DWC (Douglas World Cruiser) floatplanes in 1924.

Early in 1926, Major Franco, a brother of General Francisco Franco, made the first east–west crossing of the South Atlantic to Buenos Aires, Argentina, from Palos de Magues, Spain, in a Dornier Wal. For this date, it was a great accomplishment to fly almost 6300 miles (10 140 km) in less than 60 hr flying time. In August 1930, Wolfgang Von Grunau successfully crossed the North Atlantic from Germany via Iceland, Greenland and New York and then on to Chicago. What is even more remarkable is the fact that this was one of the two aircraft used by Roald Amundsen in his attempt to reach the North Pole in 1925 and was purchased by Captain Frank H Courtney for use in his transatlantic attempt. After abandoning the project following two unsuccessful attempts in 1925, the same aircraft was purchased by Grunau, who made the flight in August 1930.

A contemporary competitor of the Dornier Wal was the Rhorbach Ro II (1923) which featured a very angular design, concentrating on large, flat plate surfaces rather than multicurvature design. The hull was very angular with sharp chines and longerons joining rectangular frames and bulkheads. This framework was covered by flat sheets of aluminium on the top and sides. The hull bottom surface was another matter. Here, the surface was formed in a concave contour between the deep V keel and the chines. The shape was carefully plotted to give a sharp cleavage of the water on alighting and force the water to be deflected back downwards to reduce the spray pattern and provide hydrodynamic lift at the same time. The wings and tail surface of the Rhorbach aircraft were also very angular, appearing to be formed by simply wrapping a metal sheet around the leading edge and fastening together the ends at the trailing edge. The wing tips were simply flat plates conforming to the rib profile. The monoplane wing was fitted to the upper surface of the fuselage and the engines were mounted in pods attached by a steel tube truss structure above the centre section of the wing and fuselage. Stabilizing floats were structurally similar to the hull in design and were fastened to the wing lower surface close to the fuselage rather than near the wing tips as was generally done by other designers. A unique feature of the Ro III of 1924 was an emergency system consisting of two masts with sails which could be erected above the hull to sail into port or sail clear of dangerous waters or to known steamer routes if forced down at sea. The Ro IIIs were always fitted with two or more engines.

There followed from the first Ro I, II, III and IV, a series of improved aircraft which were given names of

Romar, Rocco, and Rostra, all of which looked the same in profile but varied quite considerably in size and number of powerplants. The wing planform of these named aircraft also changed from the rectangular planform of the Ro I series, but once established, this new design with tapered panels outboard of the engine or float attachment points remained virtually the same geometrically. The span and overall area varied but the shape remained constant but enlarged.

A contemporary of the Supermarine Sea Lion II and winner of the 1922 Schneider race was the Supermarine Seagull Amphibian. Although similar in general plan and profile, it was larger dimensionally with a 46-ft (14-m) span and inferior performance to that of the Sea Lion. The Seagull was a workhorse, spotter-type aircraft used mainly for photographic duties and was replaced in 1925.

Experience gained from the design of the Supermarine Swan civil transport flying boat was put to good use in the

ROHRBACH Ro III

Founded in 1922 in Copenhagen, the Rohrbach-Metall-Aeroplane Co A/S produced seaplanes which included the Ro III with its two sails. The Ro III was sold to Japan and Turkey

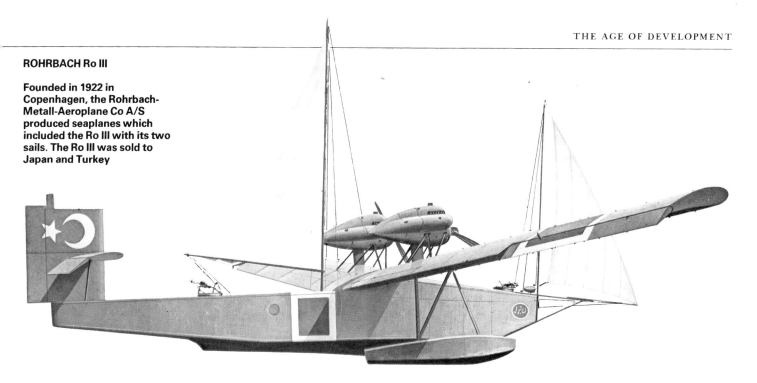

design and production of the 1925 Supermarine Southampton. It was built as a replacement for the F.5 coastal patrol aircraft which were, by this date, on their last legs. Wood hulls were still the standard construction but the Southampton had a well-rounded hull configuration which would lead one to expect speeds in excess of its actual 108 mph (174 km/h). In its original configuration, the Southampton was powered by two Napier Lion engines of 470 hp each, which were very exposed to the slipstream and probably contributed aerodynamic drag which would account for their slow speed. The hull curved gracefully upward from the rear step to a horizontal stabilizer-elevator, upon which was mounted three fins and rudders. During its working lifetime the Southampton was fitted with a variety of engines varying in power and configuration.

In the United States, where flying boats were still being produced, the Naval Aircraft Factory PNs were built in 1925 to replace the F.5Ls then in operation with the US Navy. The PN-8s were metal-hulled aircraft, powered by 475-hp Packard engines. With redesign of the tail surfaces, they were designated PN-9s. On 1 September, 1925 Commander John Rogers, US Naval Aviator, and a crew of four, attempted to make the first non-stop flight from San Francisco to Honolulu, flying a PN-9. They were forced to land out of fuel and 450 miles (724 km) short of their destination, having flown 1841.12 miles (2962.9 km) before landing. After ten days afloat, they were sighted ten miles (16 km) from their destination by a submarine which was part of a massive search team. Commander Rogers and his crew had made a sail out of wing fabric and proceeded to sail the PN-9 on toward their destination. In spite of failure to reach the intended goal, the non-stop distance was itself a record not exceeded for another five years.

The Blackburn Iris was developed in response to an Air Ministry specification and, though produced in limited

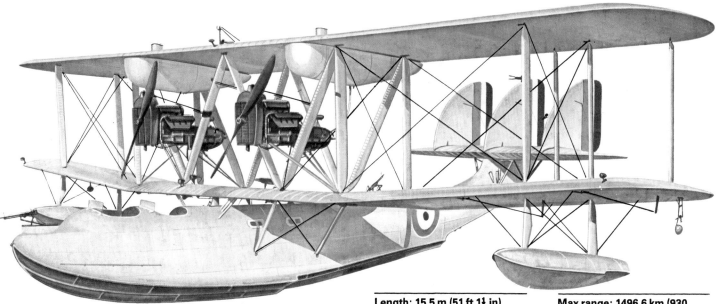

SUPERMARINE SOUTHAMPTON

Famous as an inter-war 'flag carrier', the Southampton

served with the RAF for over a decade

Span: 22.8 m (75 ft)

Length: 15.5 m (51 ft 1¼ in)

Engine: 2 502 hp Napier Lion Vs

Max speed: 173.8 km/h (108 mph)

Max range: 1496.6 km (930 miles)

Armament: 3 Lewis machine-guns and 498 kg (1100 lb) of bombs

The prototype Blackburn Iris V, this was an Iris III fitted with 825 hp Rolls-Royce Buzzard IIMS V-type engines. The Iris development programme in the late 20s paved the way for types which later saw action in World War II

quantity, was one of the largest aircraft of that decade. It had a wing span of 97 ft (29.5 m) which was 5 ft (1.5 m) greater than the H-12 Large America of World War I. A slow evolutionary development programme for the Iris was carried out during its operational life span. This was the era of transition from wood to metal structures and the Iris was swept along with this tide. The Iris II replaced the wood hull of the Iris I with a metal sheathed hull. Along with this transition in construction materials came an improvement in engine design and power. The original 650-hp Rolls-Royce Condor engines were replaced by 825-hp Rolls-Royce Buzzard engines for the Iris III. The Iris VI, built in 1933, was larger and was powered by Rolls-Royce Buzzard engines and became the prototype of the Perth.

During the long development period of the Iris in the UK, flying boats and amphibians and smaller flying craft were developed in the United States. Among these, the Loening OLs were developed as versatile, if ungainly looking, amphibians. One of these Loenings, the OL-9, a development of the earlier OL-2, was used for extensive exploration work by the 1925 MacMillan expedition on Labrador. One of the members of the crew of this little known expedition was a man who was to become famous as an explorer in the Antarctic, Richard E Byrd. The design, according to Grover Loening, was calculated from the outset to make US Army pilots, who had endured long years operating weary DH-4s, feel at home. The location of the pilot's cockpit in relation to the wings and engine was exactly the same as in the DH-4s. The idea was good and worked with the line pilots, but they were not responsible for purchasing the replacement aircraft.

The first order for the Loening amphibians was the result of an accident. General William Mitchel was making an inspection tour of the country in a DH-4 when, in the vicinity of the Mississippi River, his engine died. He was forced to make a dead-stick landing in the river and the swim that followed prompted Mitchel to place an immediate order for five machines.

The water-cooled engines of the earlier Loening amphibian models were replaced by radial air-cooled Pratt & Whitney Wasp engines, changing the designation to OL-8 and finally to OL-9. The Loenings generally were utility aircraft and were well regarded as staff aircraft and for exploration expeditions. Five OA-1As, which were basically the same as the OL-9s but fitted with inverted Liberty engines, made the first South American Goodwill flight in early 1927. The same configuration, but vastly improved, was the Grumman J2F, known as the Duck, which saw service in World War II. At the end of World War II a design for a monoplane with this same hull configuration was in the test stage. It was the Columbia Aircraft Corporation, XJ-1, a refined version of the OL series aircraft. Structurally, the Loenings were interesting in that they used fabric covered wings almost identical to the DH-4s of World War I and the postwar years and had a wood fuselage structure with aluminium sheets screwed to the frame giving the outward appearance of an all-metal fuselage.

In the early 1920s there were companies who specialized in marine aircraft, notably Shorts, Blackburn and Supermarine in Britain; Dornier and Rhorbach in Germany; Macchi and Savoia-Marchetti in Italy; Breguet and Latécoère in France; and Sikorsky, Boeing, Martin and Consolidated in the United States. While other manufacturers in each of these countries built an occasional flying boat, these companies persisted in developing a progressing line of flying boats, steadily improving the hydrodynamics of this type of aircraft along with the progress in aerodynamics and powerplants. During this era of pro-

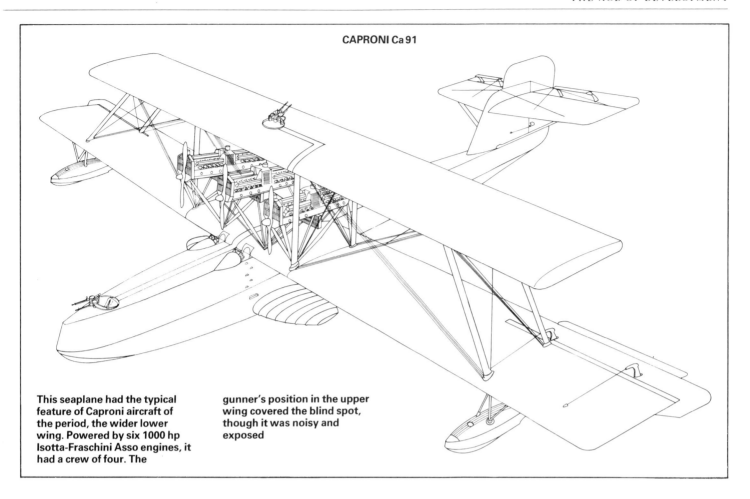

CAPRONI Ca 91

This seaplane had the typical feature of Caproni aircraft of the period, the wider lower wing. Powered by six 1000 hp Isotta-Fraschini Asso engines, it had a crew of four. The gunner's position in the upper wing covered the blind spot, though it was noisy and exposed

peller-driven flying boats, two design characteristics had to be reckoned with in each design. One was the necessity to mount the engine(s) and propeller(s) in a position high enough to keep the propeller clear of the spray pattern generated by the aircraft movement through the water. The other design characteristic was the requirement for a stabilizing flotation for lateral stability when on or in contact with the water surface. Each company approached these requirements in a slightly different way. Some increased the depth of the hull, others mounted the engines above the fuselage or wing, others mounted the engines between the wing panels and still others mounted the engines in the leading edge of the wing and then with a pylon or other structural means mounted the wing and engines high above the hull. The float design and attachment followed a similar pattern, but one company, Dornier, chose to make the flotation unit do double duty. By attaching what appeared to be a stub wing outward from the chines, they attained a flotation unit and, in addition, a source of aerodynamic lift as well as a planing surface. This was a very efficient way to cover all requirements. The same design feature was later used by Martin, Consolidated and Boeing.

Igor Sikorsky, a Russian by birth, emigrated to the United States following the Soviet Revolution, bringing with him a penchant for large aircraft. He also surrounded himself with a number of White Russian expatriates who merged comfortably into their new homeland and built a steady stream of successful flying boats and amphibians. Along the route they built the twin-engined S-38 which was followed by the single-engined S-39. Probably the best known pair of these aircraft were the S-38 and S-39 operated by the explorer/film producer team of Osa and Martin Johnson who, through the medium of film, gave many of us our first sight of what we used to call the 'Dark

Continent'. The Johnsons' planes, painted with a zebra pattern camouflage, were always in the films. These two amphibian aircraft were of the type which had the engine(s) mounted in the wing leading edge and the wing mounted high above the hull. They also had the tail surfaces mounted on tail booms well above the water spray. They resembled the configuration of the Sopwith Bat Boat and the NC boats of transatlantic fame. The Sikorskys saw extensive use in exploration and route pioneering and survey flights in the Caribbean, up South American rivers and along the Alaskan coast as well as in Africa.

Later, an immense aircraft for its day, the four-engined Sikorsky S-40, followed the same design pattern to become one of the earliest airline service-type aircraft to inaugurate passenger and mail service from the US to South America. A refinement and enlargement of these early designs was the S-42 which dropped the Bat Boat configuration and extended the hull further to the rear providing additional hull capacity and eliminating the requirement for tail booms. The tail surfaces were mounted on the extreme rear structure of the hull, as in the case of the Curtiss H-1 America of 1914.

The Caproni Ca 91, a large flying boat of mixed construction, was derived from the Ca 90 land-plane and, like the Dornier Wal, used a small sponson in addition to wing-tip floats for stability on the water and to provide an extra planing surface. Some idea of the size of this machine can be gained by the fact that its six engines, three tractor and three pushers, totalled 6000 hp. It carried a defensive gunner, sitting in a cockpit installed in the upper wing centre section and was armed with a pair of mounted machine guns. The bow and dorsal gun positions were similarly equipped.

With a steady pace toward full metalization of aircraft, the Hall Aluminum Company was awarded a contract for

HALL PH-3

With a crew of four this flying boat was designed in the 1920s but was still in service with the Coast Guard in World War II.

Span: 22.25 m (72 ft 10 in)

Length: 15.5 m (51 ft)

Engine: 2 875 hp Wright R-1820-F51 9-cylinder radials

Max speed: 255.8 km/h (159 mph)

Max range: 3701.4 km (2300 miles)

Armament: 4 90-kg (200-lb) or 113-kg (250-lb) depth bombs

construction of a Naval Aircraft Factory (US) design based almost entirely on the PN-11 biplane flying boat. The exception and difference in design related principally to the fin and rudder which were enlarged to obtain greater directional stability. The PH, as the design was designated, featured a two-step all-metal hull and was powered by two 537-hp Wright GR1750 engines. The PH-2, an improved model, was ordered by the US Coast Guard. They were fitted with more powerful engines, the 750-hp Wright R1920F-51 and Coast Guard operating equipment. A further refinement of the design produced the PH-3 with NACA ring cowls and long chord nacelles for the engines. The biplane PH-3s were in service right up to World War II. Following the Pearl Harbor attack, when the US Coast Guard automatically became a component of the US Navy, they donned the standard navy finish and took their place on the submarine patrol circuit. The monoplane flying boat designs were in development and procurement phase by this time, making the Hall PH series obsolete.

One of the types to move the biplane flying boats along the road to obsolescence was the Consolidated Commodore which, like the Hall PHs, was introduced in 1929. A high wing monoplane with angular hull lines, the Commodore was used by the New York, Rio and Buenos Aires Airline to begin the service of what was later to become Pan American Airways. With 12 Commodore aircraft, service was inaugurated between the United States and South America in 1929. The NYRBA Airline was absorbed by Pan American in 1930, along with a number of other existing and competing airlines, to create a service from Miami to Buenos Aires which connected 15 nations en route through the Caribbean and down the eastern coast of South America. By this time, it was recognized by airline economists on both sides of the Atlantic that one of the keys to successful airline operation was the ability to carry enough passengers and mail and be able to break even with something less than a 100% load factor. Aircraft the size of the Commodore, with a capacity of 18 seats, were adequate for the pioneering phase but the price of a ticket had to be increased or the cost of the operation had to come down. If

greater numbers of passengers were to be found, the price had to be reduced making it necessary to go the route of greater capacity and greater efficiency of operation.

One of the most noteworthy, even spectacular, attempts in the direction of greater seat capacity was the Dornier Do-X, also built in 1929. A giant of its day, the Do-X was designed to carry up to 170 passengers on segments of the Atlantic routes. As in so many cases before and since, the Do-X was an overly optimistic design, which was plagued with problems during its short operational life. On a trip from Amsterdam via Lisbon, Rio de Janeiro and Miami to New York, the Do-X was dogged by troubles and took from 2 November, 1930 until 27 August, 1931 to complete the trip. One of the problems was insufficiently powerful engines. This resulted in the installation of no less than 12 engines in six combination pusher/tractor engine nacelles, mounted atop the massive monoplane wing. A variety of engines were tried but the problems normally experienced with even one engine of that period, would seem to make this installation a built-in source of trouble. Its gargantuan dimensions guaranteed front page space if only to tell of its persistent problems.

One of the few instances when the Douglas Aircraft Company ventured into the flying boat field resulted in the design and limited production of a ruggedly handsome amphibian named the Dolphin which was a compact, seaworthy machine used extensively by the US Coast Guard. At least one plane was fitted out as an executive-type aircraft and the US Army ordered 21 Dolphins under designations C-21, C-26, YIC-26A, C-26B and C-29A, all of which were based on the engines installed. They ranged from 300-hp Wasp Jrs to 575-hp Pratt & Whitney R-1340s and included Wright R-975 engines of 350 hp. US Navy orders amounted to 27 units under RD designations which changed to RD-2 when the 450-hp Pratt & Whitney R1340-9 Wasp engines were installed. One of the peculiarities of the US Coast Guard procurement through the years is that their aircraft have been ordered by the US Navy, therefore, many of the Dolphins ordered by the navy were actually operated by the Coast Guard. In December 1941,

The Dornier Do X suffered from a number of mechanical problems and minor disasters during its service, but has the distinction of being the first aircraft to carry 169 passengers—as far back as 1929. It was however intended to carry between 66 and 72 passengers who travelled in great luxury. In 1930 the Do X went on a world trip which took it to New York via South America.
Bottom: The Do X with its 169 crew and passengers including nine stowaways

the Coast Guard was absorbed into the navy for the duration of World War II and the Dolphins were assigned to submarine security patrols along the Atlantic coast of the United States. Only one Dolphin is known to survive today, and that is privately owned by Colgate Darden.

In 1930, the Saro (for Saunders-Roe) A.19 Cloud appeared on the horizon and, like the Dolphin, had a wooden wing and an aluminium hull. In general, it was a scaled up, refined edition of an earlier Saunders-Roe aircraft, the Cutty Sark, and was similar in configuration to the Douglas Dolphin and a contemporary Fokker BIV whose wood wing design was used on all four aircraft. All of these interesting machines were amphibious but none had fully retracting wheels. Each merely lifted the wheels sufficiently high to clear the surface when flown from or onto the water.

The naval aircraft design series of twin-engined biplane flying boats came to an end with the PN-12 aircraft. At the same time, by reason of corporate mergers, the manufacture of these aircraft came full cycle. Production of the naval aircraft design was awarded to Keystone Aircraft

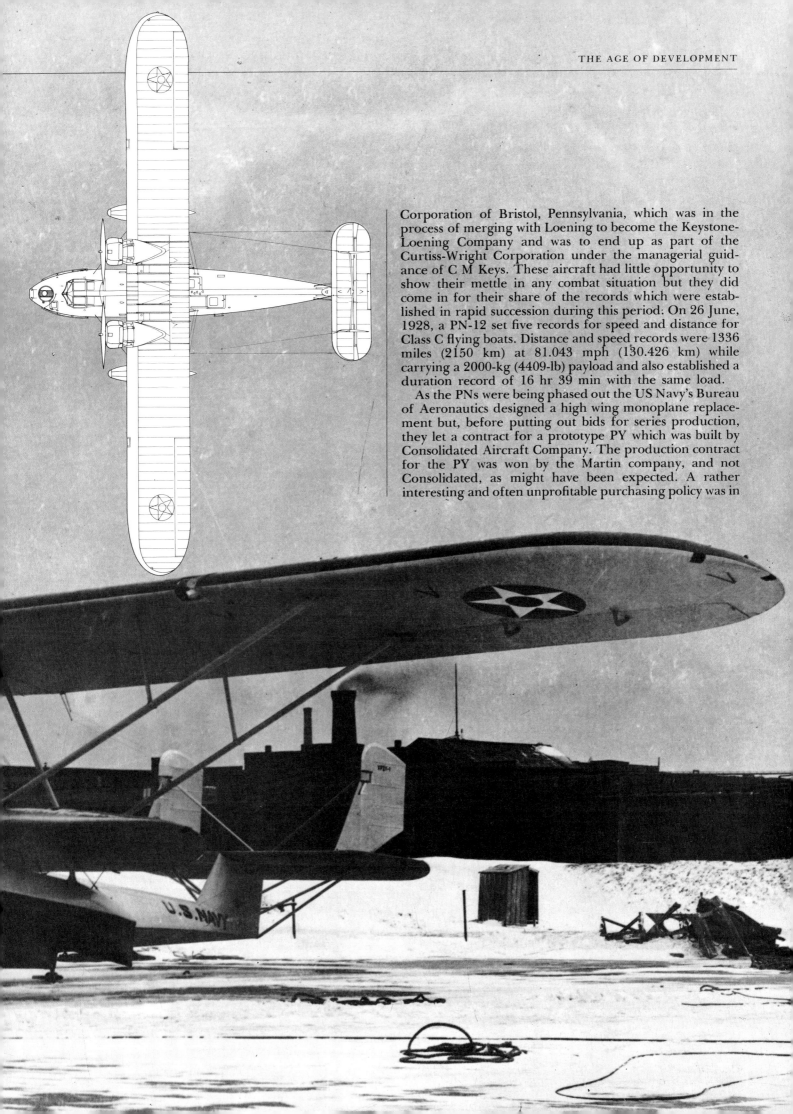

Corporation of Bristol, Pennsylvania, which was in the process of merging with Loening to become the Keystone-Loening Company and was to end up as part of the Curtiss-Wright Corporation under the managerial guidance of C M Keys. These aircraft had little opportunity to show their mettle in any combat situation but they did come in for their share of the records which were established in rapid succession during this period: On 26 June, 1928, a PN-12 set five records for speed and distance for Class C flying boats. Distance and speed records were 1336 miles (2150 km) at 81.043 mph (130.426 km) while carrying a 2000-kg (4409-lb) payload and also established a duration record of 16 hr 39 min with the same load.

As the PNs were being phased out the US Navy's Bureau of Aeronautics designed a high wing monoplane replacement but, before putting out bids for series production, they let a contract for a prototype PY which was built by Consolidated Aircraft Company. The production contract for the PY was won by the Martin company, and not Consolidated, as might have been expected. A rather interesting and often unprofitable purchasing policy was in

The forward gun position in a Blackburn Perth showing the 37-mm (1.46-in) COW gun with a coaxial machine-gun and anchor slung under the bow

effect at this time which nearly bankrupted the aircraft manufacturers in the United States. It was in keeping with the US services' mandate to get the most for the taxpayers' dollar through the means of minimum cost purchasing contracts. There were many pros and cons to this practice, discussions of which are beyond the scope of this brief survey. The sting of losing the production contract for the PY model to Martin was partially offset by Consolidated receiving a contract to develop a second version, designated the P2Y. Using the same main wing and adding a half-span lower wing, the P2Y became a sesquiplane with the early Wright R-1820E engines mounted in the leading edge of the upper wing centre section in the P2Y-2 version. The lower wing provided an attachment structure for the stabilizing floats which, on the earlier PY model, were supported by a truss structure which served no other purpose. The sesqui wing of the P2Y contributed to the overall lift of the aircraft rather than just contributing extra drag. The P2Ys became a testing ground for mounting engines. First, two engines were mounted just under the upper wing with a third mounted above the wing, a repeat of experiments carried out on the original Curtiss H-1 American in 1914 using OX-5 engines. In 1933, the navy ordered 23 P2Y-3s which had their Wright R-1820 engines mounted in the wing leading edge. Experience gained on these aircraft was to be useful in the design of the Model 28 which was to gain fame as the PBY – Catalina of World War II fame.

During the period of the early 1930s, efforts were being made in the USSR to convert their aviation from a dependence on foreign designs.

One of the designs which was produced in quantity, exceeding 1500 aircraft and used extensively during this development period, was the Beriev MBR-2. It was a short-range single-engine monoplane which was first tested in 1931 and was still in production during World War II. Reversing the western designers' approach, the Beriev was built with a metal wing and a wood hull, whereas western designers developed the metal hulls to prevent their soaking up large quantities of water which increased the empty weight of the aircraft. Possibly the Soviet designers had learned something new in wood preservation or operated with the same load regardless of the gross weight. In its transport role, the Beriev carried eight passengers and was designated MP-1 and was the work-horse of the Soviet air fleet. As in present Soviet aircraft, they were designed as dual purpose vehicles – military and civil.

As noted in the description of the Blackburn Iris, the Perth was the service replacement aircraft. The Iris IV was, in fact, the prototype of the Perth. At this stage, transition from wood to metal structure was achieved though the metal wings were fabric covered. They were still biplanes and continued in service until 1937, though they were made obsolescent much earlier by the acceptance of the Short Singapore III in April, 1935. First delivery of a Singapore was made by Squadron Leader Plendeleith who had been the pilot of one of the earlier leading contenders for the first round-the-world flight. The Singapores were used largely to show the flag in the eastern Mediterranean, Far East and, when the Spanish Civil War broke out, to ensure the safety of British shipping. The Singapore,

BLACKBURN PERTH

The Perth was the largest biplane flying boat to serve with the RAF. It entered service in 1934 and differed from the Iris by having an enclosed cockpit

Span: 29.5 m (97 ft)

Length: 21.3 m (70 ft)

Engines: 3 825 hp Rolls-Royce Buzzards

Max speed: 212 km/h (132 mph)

Range: 1445 km (898 miles)

Armament: 3 or 4 Lewis machine-guns and 907 kg (2000 lb) of bombs

Short Singapore flying boats operating from Alexandria in a prewar antipiracy patrol. On normal operations they had a range of 1609 km (1000 miles). Some aircraft were still in service at the outbreak of World War II.

Caught in the winter sunlight over Pembroke Dock a Supermarine Stranraer circles over a moored aircraft. Stranraers entered service in 1936 and the last was withdrawn in 1943 after operating with the RCAF in a coastal reconnaissance role

because of its ample cruising range, had complete live-aboard facilities, a 'luxury' often enjoyed by flying boat crews from this time forward. The last Singapore was completed in mid-1937 and remained active until well into World War II.

A contemporary Italian flying boat design was the Savoia-Marchetti S-55 which was unusual in appearance. It reverted back to the Bat Boat configuration, with a short hull and the tail surfaces mounted on tail booms only this time a new wrinkle was added – twin hull, booms and engines all attached to a monoplane wing. This configuration eliminated the need for the wing-tip floats.

In Britain, about the same time, another flying boat, the Saunders-Roe London, was being built which was tailored to the RAF's requirement for long-range flying boats which could, in reasonable time, bring air power to any point in the British Empire. To demonstrate this ability, the RAF mounted long-range cruises to the far ends of the Empire. Such was the case when the Londons were received and operationally shaken-down. In December, 1937, a flight of Londons was dispatched to New South Wales. By the time they returned, they had covered a distance equal to that of the Italian armada. The London was pressed into service in 1939 for the North Sea patrol, to fill in until their replacement Sunderlands were available in sufficient quan-

tity to cover the vast areas dominated by German submarine operations. As was the custom at this time, these Londons like so many of the immediate predecessors, were produced in limited numbers compared to their successor Sunderlands.

At about the same time in the early 1930s, another great flying boat was making its debut – the Sikorsky S-42. The Sikorsky was to be the long-range replacement for the pioneering Sikorsky S-40 which was of the Bat Boat, NC-4 configuration but on a much larger scale. The S-42, on the other hand, had an elongated fuselage, in contrast to the S-40, and was an all metal structure, with the wing fitted on a streamlined pylon above the hull. Four air-cooled Pratt & Whitney Hornet engines of 750 hp each were mounted in the leading edge of the wing producing a maximum speed of 188 mph (302.5 km/h), and a range of 1200 miles (1930 km). With this range and a gross take-off weight of 42 000 lb (19 050 kg), the S-42 was one of the most important stepping stones in the development of Pan American Airways.

The Supermarine Stranraer, which entered service in 1936, was the fastest of the biplane flying boats with the RAF. They were also the best protected, in a structural sense, taking advantage of the preserving characteristics of the anodising process then being introduced. It was

Left: A Sikorsky JRS-1 (Y10A-8) amphibian which was used by the US Navy and USAAF during World War II. It could carry 15 passengers and was powered by two 750 hp Pratt & Whitney radial engines.
Below: A Short S18 'Knuckleduster' which first flew in November 1933. The type was never operational, but was important in monoplane flying boat design

SARO LONDON I

Powered by two 1000 hp Bristol Pegasus engines the Saro London had a crew of six and was armed with three .303-in (7.7-mm) machine-guns. It had a maximum speed of 249.4 km/h (155 mph)

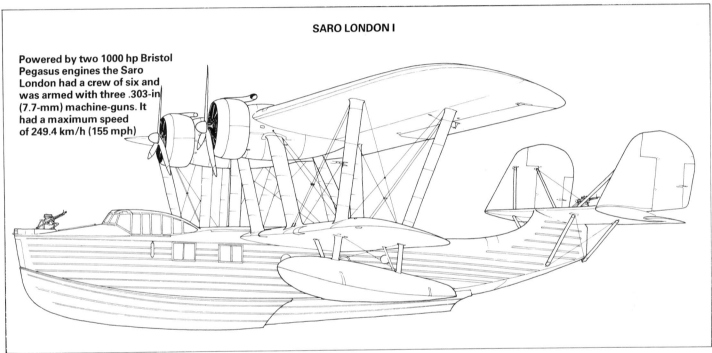

SUPERMARINE STRANRAER

Span:	25.9 m (85 ft)
Length:	16.7 m (54 ft 10 in)
Engine:	2 920 hp Bristol Pegasus
Max speed:	241 km/h (150 mph)
Endurance:	9.6 hours

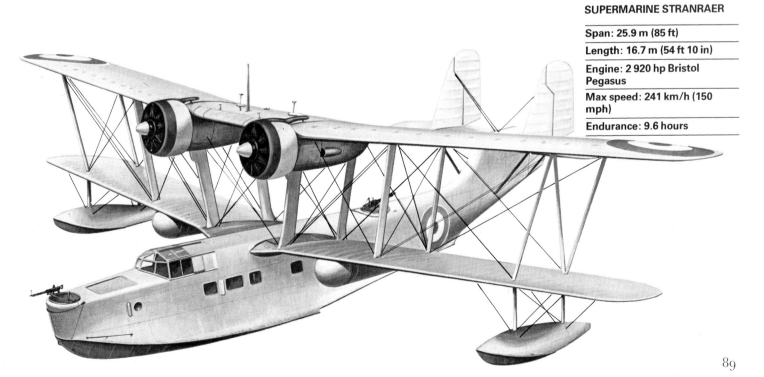

particularly advantageous to marine aircraft which were always subject to corrosion from sea water. It is at least partially responsible for the survival of one beautifully restored example exhibited in the RAF Museum at Hendon. The Stranraer was a development from the Southampton, a 1925 aircraft designed by R J Mitchell, whose best-known designs were the Supermarine S6B, winner of the Schneider Trophy and the world-famous World War II fighter, the Spitfire. The Stranraers were also produced and operated in Canada, serving in the RCAF until replaced by Canso PBYs in 1943.

The mid-30s produced a variety of flying boats. They were and still are one of the best vehicles for service in remote areas where acres of concrete runways are not practical for economic and environmental reasons. Their ability to use almost any reasonable body of water for operations was a very useful characteristic before World War II brought with it the construction of airfields in most strategically important parts of the world.

An amphibian, carrying forward the Loening and Keystone-Loening configuration was the Grumman J2F Duck. Like the Loenings, the Duck was an unusual 'spoon bill' amphibian with the bow of the single float projecting under and well forward of the propeller. It owed some of its parentage to a Curtiss flying boat built in 1913 for Harold F McCormick. The same configuration was used by Loening who added a retractable landing gear to make it amphibious and extended its utility considerably. The Duck was a single-engined aircraft with biplane wings of equal span. During World War II they were used most advantageously as a general utility aircraft and, on occasion, as a submarine hunter. In spite of its rather ungainly appearance, it was much used and found to be a good target-towing and search-rescue aircraft for close inshore areas. It was a three-place machine having accommodation for pilot, radioman, and mechanic-gunner, all within the confines of its long greenhouse canopy and in the fuselage above the float structure. Only a few of these aircraft survive and are now in private hands or with brokers. They were powered by the Wright R-1820-F52 Cyclone engine which, initially, was rated at 775 hp. They gradually increased in power as the war progressed, and the need for a jack-of-all-trades utility aircraft.

In France there was also continuing development of flying boats. As early as 1931-34 some very interesting and attractive designs appeared. Among this group was the

Bleriot 5190, designed to be a transatlantic monoplane transport type; the Breguet Bizerte and Saïgon long-range reconnaissance and commercial flying boats which were developments of the Short Calcutta; and the Loire 70, a reconnaissance monoplane flying boat with a peculiar three-engine installation consisting of the outboard 550-hp Gnome-Rhône radial engines mounted in a tractor configuration and the centre engine in a pusher configuration. Liore-et-Oliver fielded a group of four flying boats; the single-engined sesquiplane amphibian reconnaissance H-23-2, the H-199, a twin-engined biplane commercial design and the H-24-2 and H-27, both of which were four-engined monoplane commercial aircraft. Latécoère was just as prolific as Liore-et-Oliver, producing a group of machines which had a distinct resemblance to the Dornier Wal with sponsons instead of stabilizing wing-tip floats. Of the group, the Latécoère 30-1, a four-engined long-range mail plane, was aesthetically the most attractive. It also was designed for transatlantic service. One of these aircraft, christened Croix du Sud, established a distance record on 1 January, 1934, by flying from Berre Lake, in France, to Senegal, a distance of 2357 miles (3793 km). This flight and a following flight from Senegal to Natal, Brazil created

quite a stir and aroused the interest of the French navy. Three 30-2s, a military version based on the 30-1, were purchased by the navy as long-range reconnaissance machines. Eventually, one of the commercial 30-1s was also acquired by the navy and modified for military purposes. These four aircraft operated until they were grounded due to lack of spares, The last continued to operate until the spring of 1941 by cannibalizing parts from other aircraft.

About this same time Soviet design teams were beginning to show the results of their efforts to convert from dependency on foreign aircraft manufacturers to domestic production although they still maintained licences to produce certain foreign aircraft and components. Unfortunately, a number of aircraft designers were working under conditions scarcely conducive to the production of good designs. Both Tupolev and Grigorovitch were incarcerated for long periods of time 'for sabotage'. During their imprisonment, they and their design team continued their design efforts but it could be expected to be less imaginative than had these designers been working unrestricted.

In 1935, the ARK-3, developed by I N Chetverikov, was produced as a multipurpose flying boat and designed to meet the needs of the undeveloped miles of Soviet territ-

Above: The French Loire 70 reconnaissance flying boat takes off from St Nazaire for a patrol.
Left: The Short Calcutta during its trials at Rochester in February 1928. The Medway was a major flying boat base before and during the war

The Short-Mayo Composite also known as Mercury and Maia. The design allowed the smaller Mercury to be lifted to an effective cruising height without expending large amounts of fuel. As a result she was able to make record-breaking flights to South Africa and the United States. The design became obsolete with the development of in-flight refuelling techniques. The first composite flight was made on 20 January 1938 and the first commercial flight in July 1938

ory. The first requirement was for a reconnaissance aircraft to complete the mapping of thousands of square miles of land, particularly in the northern reaches of the country. Secondarily, a transport version was required. The transport version could carry up to 12 passengers in reasonable comfort. A monoplane with a two-stepped hull, it was powered by two 700-hp M-25V air-cooled radial engines mounted in tandem on a pylon above the wing centre section. It was a robust machine with good perform-ance. In April, 1937, the type established a record for height and weight of 30 151 ft (9190 m), carrying a 1000-kg (2204-lb) payload. As late as World War II these aircraft were being used to patrol convoys in the northern ocean areas.

Close on the heels of the ARK was a replacement aircraft, the Beriev MDR-6 (Be-4) which was put into production just in time for the outbreak of World War II

in 1939. It, like the ARK-3, was a twin-engined monoplane with a two-stepped hull. In this aircraft, the engines were mounted on the leading edge of the wing in nicely faired cowls. The powerplants, 9-cylinder M-63 radial engines, developing 1100 hp, were derived from the Wright Cy-clone 9 engine, licence-built in the USSR. During World War II this aircraft was improved by installation of 12-cylinder liquid-cooled Vlimov M195A engines which were capable of being further developed for increased power. The initial conversion showed an increase in performance which was a bonus and, with each stage of development of the engine, the performance of the MDR-6 was corres-pondingly increased. In appearance the MDR-6s bore striking resemblance to the Grumman Goose amphibian but dimensionally they were larger than the Goose.

The latter half of the 1930s saw the design and early testing of the flying boats that were to be the mainstays of the flying fleets of World War II. Among these were such famous designs as the Short Sunderlands, Supermarine Walrus, Consolidated PBY Catalina, Dornier 18, Kawanishi H6K5 (type 97) Mavis and others.

As early as 1936 the Short Sunderlands were being built. Their design was based on the C class Empire flying boats which formed the backbone of Britain's Imperial Airways. The C class aircraft operated before and during the war with some surviving the war. It was a C class flying boat that inaugurated the Imperial Airways/BOAC transatlantic ser-vice on 8 August, 1939, just weeks before the outbreak of World War II. Eventually the G type boats, a larger version of the C types, were added to the fleet but, due to war necessities, were not produced in large quantity. Instead, production and development were concentrated on the Sunderland.

One interesting facet of the C type was the single type constructed for the Short-Mayo Composite experiments. This single aircraft, christened Maia, had a greater planing bottom with a wider flare at the bow, to lift the increased weight and area of both the wing and tail surfaces. In addition, the outboard engines were more widely spaced to accommodate the Mercury, a twin-float, four-engined aircraft which was mounted on a frame above the centre of the wing of Maia. The spacing accommodated the floats of the Mercury and also increased the wing area. Operation-ally, the Maia served to lift the Mercury to cruising altitude, at which time they would separate after the Mercury showed a positive lift capability, allowing the Mercury to proceed to destination fully laden. One trip was made from Foynes, Ireland, to Montreal, non-stop on 21 July, 1938. A second flight, on 6 October, was made from Dundee to South Africa, a distance of 9728 km (6044.7 miles), to establish an international distance record for seaplanes. While it was considered to be a practical system for transport of high priority cargo and mail, the war inter-vened and flight refuelling later became a practical opera-tional technique requiring less technical support equip-ment. The remarkable feature of this experiment is that this aircraft accomplished these records with so little power, the Mercury being equipped with four Napier-Halford H Rapier Mk VI engines of less than 1000 hp each. The Maia could also be used independently of the Mercury to serve as one of the fleet of C class boats. Under

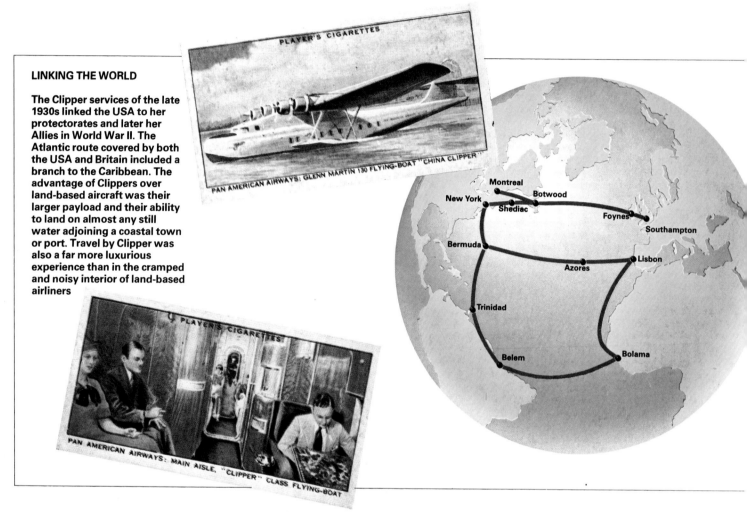

PLAYER'S CIGARETTES

PAN AMERICAN AIRWAYS: GLENN MARTIN 130 FLYING-BOAT "CHINA CLIPPER"

LINKING THE WORLD

The Clipper services of the late 1930s linked the USA to her protectorates and later her Allies in World War II. The Atlantic route covered by both the USA and Britain included a branch to the Caribbean. The advantage of Clippers over land-based aircraft was their larger payload and their ability to land on almost any still water adjoining a coastal town or port. Travel by Clipper was also a far more luxurious experience than in the cramped and noisy interior of land-based airliners

PLAYER'S CIGARETTES

PAN AMERICAN AIRWAYS: MAIN AISLE, "CLIPPER" CLASS FLYING-BOAT

these circumstances it could carry up to 24 passengers and their baggage, plus 1½ tons of mail in its spacious hull.

In the last half of the 1930s, efforts were being made in the USA to establish air routes to the Pacific Islands and the Philippine Islands which, at that time, were under the protection of the United States. To do this, it was necessary to use flying boats since land-based airports were still a long way off. At least it seemed so, for it was not until World War II that military necessity created the need for landing strips on many Pacific Islands. The flight of the PN-9 and, subsequently, the successful non-stop flight of Maitland and Hagenberger to Hawaii on 1 June, 1927, was the forging of the first link in the chain that would eventually span the Pacific on a regular service basis. To push the chain farther west required the development of a flying boat with greater range. The design for this project, sponsored by Pan American Airways, was the Martin M-130 Clipper. The name Clipper was a rebirth of the name used by the famed high-speed sailing ships that had originally tied these far-flung islands to the North American continent. The routes had been surveyed by Captain Edwin C Musick and crew in the Sikorsky S-42 aircraft which had previously given good service on Caribbean routes of Pan American. When completed, the three Martin Clippers were named China Clipper, Hawaiian Clipper and Philippine Clipper.

Full transpacific service began on 21 October, 1936, and took five or six days since rest stops were included in the

schedule. Routing was from San Francisco via Hawaii, Midway, Wake, Guam, Manila and finally extended to Hong Kong in April, 1937. The Clippers provided luxury accommodations for the 12 passengers in the spacious hull. Passenger load was limited due to the large quantity of fuel required for the long stage lengths between island bases. An even larger aircraft, of similar geometry, was proposed and built, the model M-156, in 1937. It was a look-alike of the M-130 except for the tail surfaces which consisted of a single horizontal tailplane with dual fin-rudders at the outboard ends. This design did not find acceptance in US airline service. It was, however, sold to the USSR. With the exception of the Hawaiian Clipper which was lost at sea, the M-130s gave long and excellent service, like the Empire Class C boats. The M-130s averaged 5½ hr daily service, each accumulating 10 000 hr flying time and nearly 13 million passenger miles. With the beginning of the war, the Clippers were pressed into service by the US Navy for transport duties.

The follow-on for the Pacific as well as the Atlantic routes was the Boeing 314 Yankee Clipper, a deep-hulled, four-engined flying boat with three vertical fins and rudders. Twelve of these aircraft were built which were used by Pan American Airways and later by BOAC to serve the North Atlantic route and by Pan American in the Pacific throughout the war. On 20 May, 1938, Pan American began the transatlantic service. Because of wartime security, little was heard of the night flights of these

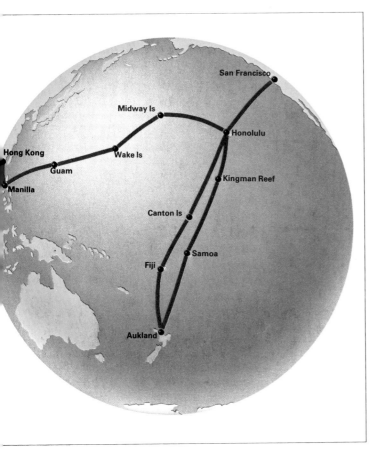

CRDA CANT Z501 GABBIANO

This aircraft sports the striking colour scheme adopted by the 184a Squadriglia Ricognizione Marittima. The Gabbiano (Gull) had a crew of four or five and operated as a light reconnaissance bomber

Span: 22.50 m (73 ft 9¾ in)

Length: 14.30 m (46 ft 11 in)

Engine: 1 900 hp Isotta-Fraschini Asso XI R2 C15 12-cylinder Vee-type

Max speed: 275 km/h (171 mph)

Max range: 2400 km (1490 miles)

Armament: 3 7.7-mm Breda-SAFAT machine-guns and 640 kg (1410 lb) of bombs

aircraft, but they served all through the war years, crossing both Atlantic and Pacific oceans on a fairly regular schedule. After the war years they continued to serve until replacement parts became a problem. They were gradually supplemented and then replaced by land-based Douglas DC-4 and Lockheed L-049 Constellations. They were sold off to non-scheduled carriers who continued to operate them for several years. Like the Martin M-130s, the Boeing 314s were shoulder-wing monoplanes, designed with sponsons like the Dornier Wals of several years earlier. The M-130 was powered by Pratt & Whitney R-1830 engines of 830 hp, while the Boeing 314s used four 1600-hp twin-row Wright Cyclone 14 engines.

The Italians have a long history of waterborne aircraft as is well known and represented by the performance and variety of aircraft entered in the Schneider Trophy race. A fair percentage of the entries were flying boats of the Macchi and Savoia-Marchetti companies. For the most part these aircraft were produced in limited quantities for specialized racing or training aircraft. It was 1934 before a production design was introduced in the form of the C.R.D.A. Cant Z.501 Gabbiano. In order to test this new aircraft, it was prepared for a record attempt and, in October 1934, flew from Trieste to Massawa, Eritrea, then an Italian colony, a non-stop distance of 2560 miles (4120 km) to establish a record for this class of aircraft. Again, in July 1935, a second flight from Trieste to Italian Somaliland increased the record distance to 3080 miles (4957

km). This aircraft type was to enter service with the Italian air force in 1936 and, by 1940, when Italy entered World War II, over 200 Gabbianos were on strength. They were used for patrol duties throughout the war. Armament was limited to three 7.7-mm (0.303-in) machine-guns, one in the bow, one in a cockpit in the upper side of the engine nacelle and one in the rear fuselage. Structure was entirely of wood with a fabric-covered wing and control surfaces. It was an extremely clean design for a flying boat and was powered by a single Isotta Fraschini Asso XI engine producing 900 hp, which was mounted in the leading edge of the high strut-mounted monoplane wing. The wing, in plan view, had elliptical outboard panels, very similar to the Spitfire, making it an attractive design but probably resulted in production problems. In the production configuration, with military load and appendages, its performance was reduced, most notably in range, to 620 miles (998 km).

About the same time period, an amphibian of great versatility was being developed for air-sea rescue and fleet reconnaissance duties, the Supermarine Walrus. The Walrus was a very angular single-engined biplane, and was to become well known. In addition to normal land and water operation, as might be expected of an amphibian, the Walrus was stressed for catapult launching. It was developed from the Supermarine Seagull, an earlier private venture type. The slab-sided fuselage hull was of sheet aluminium alloy and the wing consisted of stainless steel spars with wood ribs covered with fabric. In general, it was less than spectacular both in design and performance but it did the job so well that it was procured in large quantity. The original manufacturer produced 287 Walrus I aircraft and Saunders-Roe produced an additional 453 units under licence, known as the Walrus II which differed from Walrus I in having a wood hull and a 775-hp Pegasus VI engine instead of the earlier Pegasus II M.2. The Walrus served throughout the war in all theatres. In 1944, a successor, the Sea Otter, was gradually phased in to replace the Walrus. The Sea Otter was refined both in aerodynamics and hydrodynamics and was powered by an 855-hp Mercury XX engine in a tractor installation rather than the pusher configuration of the Walrus.

The Short Sunderland, one of the finest flying boats, had its beginnings in 1936 when the first order was placed for the prototype aircraft. It made its first flight in October 1937. The Sunderland benefitted from the extensive aerodynamic and hydrodynamic studies carried out during the design and construction of the Empire boats. The wartime exploits of the Sunderland are legion. Intended to serve as a coastal patrol aircraft, the Sunderland's duties ranged from long-range convoy patrols to services as a sea-rescue aircraft and as a transport. On one occasion, during the evacuation of Crete, a Sunderland was loaded until it began shipping water over the sill of a hatch opening with almost 90 persons inboard the cavernous hull. The Sunderland was, in its early mark series, powered by Bristol Pegasus engines and in the Mk V series by Pratt & Whitney R-1830 twin Wasp engines. Armament varied according to the job to be done. In one instance, at least, the aircraft were fitted with four forward-firing machine-guns aimed and fired by the pilot to counter the antiaircraft gun crews of German submarines. The Sunderland was so well armed, at least throughout the upper hemisphere, that a

graphic representation of its firepower would resemble an opened umbrella. Power operated turrets were installed in the bow, tail and dorsal positions and they were to earn the respect and nickname of Porcupine from their Luftwaffe adversaries. Note that this was all above the waterline, for below the waterline they, like most flying boats, were vulnerable.

The monoplane configuration of the Sunderland was a decided improvement over its predecessors as was the aerodynamically cleaner fuselage and improved planing hull. All these contributed, as they should, to the all-round improved performance. Contributing to the aerodynamic cleanliness of the airframe was the inboard stowage of its ordnance. The bomb racks of the Sunderland were designed to keep the bombs/depth charges inside the hull until ready for release. When in the vicinity of a target, the bomb racks could be run out under the wings in readiness for the attack. Almost everything was concentrated on the upper deck of the Sunderland's deep hull – the crew compartment, gun positions, and 2000-lb (907-kg) bomb-load. On some marks, guns were fitted in the hatches of the lower deck to deliver additional broadside firepower from these beam positions. When the Sunderland was first introduced, it was also one of the heaviest aircraft in service with an empty weight of 27 190 lb (12 333 kg) and an overload gross weight of over 50 000 lb (22 680 kg), nearly double the empty weight. One of the characteristics of flying boats was their facility to make a long run during take-off, assuming the sea condition was not beyond safe limits, and given enough time and run, they would eventually get off. This is not the case with land- or carrier-based aircraft which have a limited runway length.

The combat record of the Sunderland was impressive in its intended role of destroying enemy submarines and attacking aircraft. In all, 741 Sunderlands were produced;

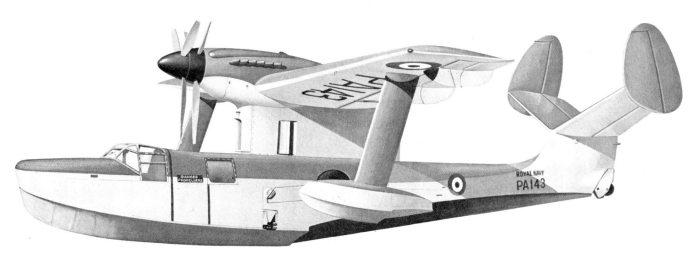

SUPERMARINE 381 'SEAGULL'

Designed as a multipurpose aircraft for both ASW and AS roles the Seagull was notable for its variable incidence wing which moved between $2\frac{1}{2}°$ and $12°$.

Span: 16 m (52 ft 6 in)	Max speed: 418 km/h (260 mph)
Length: 13.46 m (44 ft $1\frac{1}{2}$ in)	Max range: 1980 km (1230 miles)
Engine: 1 Rolls-Royce Griffin 2055 hp	

Left: A change from horse power as an elephant tows a Supermarine Walrus on an airstrip in India in 1944.
Below: A BOAC Sunderland III which was known as a Hythe class flying boat. The simple conversion involved the fairing over of the gun turrets and fitting of basic seating for the passengers. Hythe boats operated after the war until they were replaced by Sandringhams

KAWANISHI H6K1 MAVIS

This long-range maritime reconnaissance bomber entered service with the Japanese Navy in January 1938. It was used as a transport aircraft in the latter part of the war but proved very vulnerable to fighter attack since it lacked armour

Span: 40 m (131 ft 2¾ in)	
Length: 26 m (84 ft 1 in)	
Engine: 4 1300 hp Mitsubishi Kinsei 53 14-cylinder radials	

Max speed: 529 km/h (329 mph)

Endurance: 26 hours

Armament: 4 7.7-mm machine-guns, 1 20-mm cannon and up to 1995 kg (4400 lb) of bombs or torpedoes

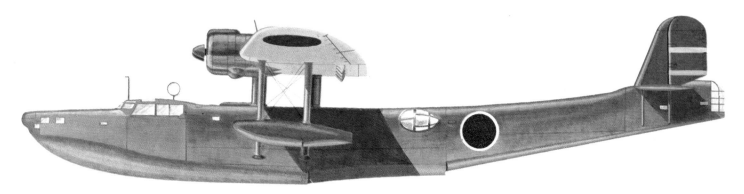

Right: An early Kawanishi H8K Emily, the fastest flying boat to serve with any of the combatants in World War II. It was also among the finest aircraft to serve with the Japanese. Well armoured and armed it had an excellent range and was treated with great respect by Allied pilots. It made its operational debut in 1942 and thereafter remained in service to the end of the war with a total of 167 aircraft being completed by 1945

240 of these were built by Blackburn Aircraft. They began their service life in 1939 and the last military Sunderland was retired in 1959. They were to live on in the service of other countries, serving with the French navy until 1960 and with the Royal New Zealand Air Force until 1966.

Derivatives of the Sunderland were the Hythes and Sandringhams which were operated by BOAC until they were sold to airline operators in New Zealand, Norway and South America.

On the other side of the world, Japan was developing its own long-range flying boats. As a maritime nation of similar geography to the UK, it was quite natural that Japan would have a strong interest in flying boats. In 1938, Japan's Kawanishi H6K-1 Mavis entered naval service after successfully passing its trials. It was an all-metal aircraft bearing a strong resemblance to the Do24 but featured fixed-wing tip floats instead of sponsons and its strut-mounted wing had a straight centre section planform with tapered outboard panels instead of the swept-back leading edge of the Do24. Instead of the three 1000-hp Bramo engines of the Dornier, the Mavis was powered initially by four 840-hp Nakajima Hikari engines. These were replaced in the production models by four 1000-hp Mitsubishi Kinsei 43 engines and finally by 1300-hp Kinsei 53 engines. It is interesting also to compare the weights of these very similar aircraft – the Dornier's empty weight being 20 062 lb (9100 kg) and the Mavis being 27 290 lb (12 380 kg). Loaded, the Dornier weighed 40 565 lb (18 400 kg) while the Mavis weighed 50 706 lb (23 000 kg). In addition to their military configuration, 18 of the H6K4-1 version were allocated to Japan Airlines for passenger services to Saipan, Palau and other Asian centres and in support of the military operations of the immediate prewar and early wartime period.

Successor to the Mavis was the Kawanishi H8K-1,

codenamed Emily by the Allied services. The design for this aircraft was begun in 1938 at the same time as the first Mavis flying boats were being accepted and tested by the Japanese navy and the Sunderland was being accepted by the RAF on the other side of the world. The similarity of appearance of the Emily and Sunderland is worth noting. The Emily did have the advantage of additional development time and, as a result, it surpassed the performance of all the Allied four-engined flying boats. Furthermore, the hydrodynamic design of the Emily was an improvement over most of its contemporaries. So advanced was the Emily that a single example was retained by the US Navy for testing purposes and still survives today at NAS Norfolk. Fortunately, financial and legal problems have been overcome, making it possible for the single surviving Emily to be returned to Japan for restoration and exhibit in a planned Japanese museum.

The otherwise clean aerodynamic design of the Emily raises questions about the fixed wing-tip floats. It was intended to have retractable floats similar to the Consolidated PB2Y Coronado and the PBY Catalina. However, the added weight of the retraction mechanism proved to be the determining factor. It was less expensive and added less weight to install fixed floats even though they were not at all in keeping with the many refinements incorporated in the remainder of the design. The maximum speed of the Emily was an impressive 251 mph (404 km/h) and the maximum range was approximately 4445 miles (7154 km), enough to cause the Allies concern, knowing these far-ranging flying boats could report the presence of the American Carrier Task Forces long before they were within striking distance of the intended target. That they did not provide this protective screen is cause for wonder about the strategy, or lack of it, shown by the Japanese navy during the Pacific war. The first production H8K1s entered service in February 1942. By the end of the war, a total of 167 Emilys had been completed.

Leaving the Marshall Islands in March 1942, three Emilys refuelled from submarine tankers in the vicinity of the French Frigate Islands about 650 miles (1046 km) from Hawaii. Although the Emily had a 27-hr endurance, it was not capable of making an unrefuelled round trip. On arrival at Hawaii, they found the islands under a heavy cloud cover and aborted their attack. It is not known if they were detected by defending forces or by radar. It is possible that a quiet watch was maintained on their movements, for this was the period when Task Force 16 was moving into position for the first air attack on Tokyo. The raid, led by Lieutenant Colonel J H Doolittle, took off from the aircraft carrier *Hornet,* and launched 16 B-25s, which flew 668 miles (1075 km) to attack Tokyo on 18 April, 1942.

Like the Sunderlands, the Emily was heavily armed with two 20-mm (0.79-in) cannons in each of the nose and tail turrets, plus a single 20-mm cannon in a dorsal turret. In addition, four 7.7-mm (0.303-in) machine-guns were carried in the side blisters and on the flight deck. As with the Mavis, a group of 30 Emilys were fitted as transports to maintain an essential communications network between the far-flung bases created by the initial fast-moving offensive of the Japanese services. They could carry over 60 passengers in this service configuration or a comparable weight in essential cargo.

The long, slender hull of the Emily makes an interesting comparison with the rather pugnacious profile of the Sunderland. It was a larger aircraft than the Sunderland, with a wing span of 124 ft 8 in (38 m) compared to the 112 ft 9½ in (34.38 m) of the Sunderland. Length was 92 ft 3½ in (28.13 m) compared to 85 ft 4 in (26 m) for the Sunderland and its take-off weight was nearly 14 000 lb (6350 kg) greater than the Sunderland. Much of this was in fuel, for its maximum endurance was nearly 27 hr, compared to nearly 14 hr for the Sunderland. The Emily was designed to operate over the long open stretches of the Pacific where endurance was an essential asset.

An aircraft more nearly comparable to the Sunderland was the Consolidated PB2Y (Model 29) Coronado, which had a wing span of 115 ft (35 m) with its wing floats in their retracted position. These floats were unique in their operation. When in their retracted position, they formed the wing tips and their supporting struts fitted into pockets faired flush with the lower surface of the wing, making an aerodynamically clean installation. This interesting design

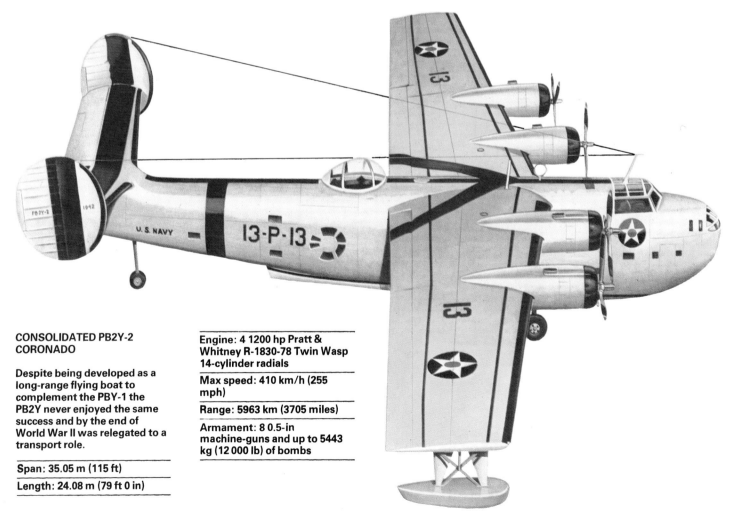

CONSOLIDATED PB2Y-2 CORONADO

Despite being developed as a long-range flying boat to complement the PBY-1 the PB2Y never enjoyed the same success and by the end of World War II was relegated to a transport role.

Span: 35.05 m (115 ft)

Length: 24.08 m (79 ft 0 in)

Engine: 4 1200 hp Pratt & Whitney R-1830-78 Twin Wasp 14-cylinder radials

Max speed: 410 km/h (255 mph)

Range: 5963 km (3705 miles)

Armament: 8 0.5-in machine-guns and up to 5443 kg (12 000 lb) of bombs

The PBY Catalina served with great distinction during World War II and was still in use with civil and military operators up to the late 1960s. Besides air-sea rescue and antisubmarine work the PBY was employed in reconnaissance and in May

1941 an RAF Catalina was instrumental in locating the German battleship *Bismarck* in the Atlantic after Royal Navy ships had lost contact. The line drawings show the PBY-5A, while the larger picture below shows a flight of prewar PBY-1s. Below: The gunner in the port beam blister position takes aim with his 0.50-in heavy machine-gun

was shared by its more famous and more numerous twin-engined contemporary, the PBY (Model 28) Catalina. The evolution of this aircraft was even more involved than that of the PBY. The wing design, with the retracting floats, remained fairly constant, but other parts of this design were changed as the aircraft developed. Though the first Coronado flew within three months after the Catalina prototype XP3Y-1, development funds for this four-engined, long-range patrol bomber were withheld until early in 1939, the bulk of available funds being allocated for PBY production, as the world moved at a breakneck pace towards World War II. Beginning life as a single-tailed four-engined machine designated XPB2Y-1, it was quickly discovered that more vertical surface area was needed on the tail. The first step in this modification process was auxiliary vertical fins at the mid-point of each horizontal stabilizer. These three fins were then replaced by a pair of circular shaped fin/rudder surfaces mounted at the outboard ends of the horizontal stabilizer. At the same time the hydrodynamic surfaces were improved by moving the second step further aft, thereby increasing the planing surface. The rather ugly bow, which incorporated a turret, was the next improvement resulting in the PB2Y-2 and, at the same time, the hull was made deeper and the rudder/fins were increased in area using surfaces of similar shape and area to those installed on the Consolidated B-24 Liberator bomber, then in large scale production. A major factor in the delayed production of these Coronados was their price tag which was approximately three times greater than the PBY. It was not until the events in Europe took on a more menacing tone that production really got under way.

For all its size and bulk, the Coronado had a good top speed of 255 mph (410 km/h) attributable in part to the retractable floats and the generally cleaned up bow and hull lines. In production, the Coronado was powered by four 1200-hp Pratt & Whitney R-1830-88 engines, a variant of the same engines that powered the PBY. The PB2Ys were produced in quantity, a total of 210 units, a number of which were converted to transport versions with low altitude R-1830 engines. Ten were turned over to the RAF to be used in transatlantic transport service. (A number of this group, probably as many as five, were eventually scuttled at sea off Bermuda at the end of the war in keeping with the lend-lease agreement under which they were obtained.) Others were converted to be used by the US Navy as ambulance planes fitted out with 25 stretchers. After the end of hostilities, all remaining Coronados were scrapped. Their service record had not been spectacular but they were scrapped not because they were poor aircraft, but mainly because their stablemate PBYs could fill the same service requirement, using only two engines and thereby reducing the fuel and maintenance requirements by nearly half.

While discussing the four-engined flying boats of this prewar and early war development period, we should not overlook one of the most useful flying boats of this period, the Boeing 314 Clipper. The Model 314 Clipper was built to fill a need for a successor to the Sikorsky S-42 and the Martin M/130 in civil airline service of Pan American Airways and later for wartime transatlantic service of

A US Navy PBY-5A roars down a crude landing strip at Amchitka on the Aleutians during US operations in January 1943. The PBY amphibians were not only able to operate from air strips and water, but could be hauled ashore if their moorings were threatened with bad weather. Catalinas were built in Canada and the United States and supplied to all the Allied air forces including the USSR

BOAC. A very clean, robust aircraft, it was powered by four 1600-hp Wright Cyclone GR-2600 engines. A high wing monoplane with Dornier-type sponsons, the 314 in the service of Pan American and BOAC maintained a regular transatlantic service all during the war.

The 314 had the distinction of transporting Prime Minister Winston Churchill home from the Bermuda Conference, and President Franklin D Roosevelt to the Casablanca Conference with Churchill. They led an interesting and well-guarded wartime service career. The seating capacity for the first six 314s was for 74, but this was increased to 77 in the second order of six aircraft, designated 314As. Of the second order placed by Pan American, three were turned over to be operated by BOAC. Almost all of the 314s survived the war in spite of a number of close encounters. The three BOAC 314 aircraft named Bristol, Berwick and Bangor were returned to the US in 1948.

Testimony to the durability of the Boeing Clippers is the fact that two were cannibalized for parts. Six were eventually scrapped in 1950 out of the dozen produced. Two were destroyed after landing at sea under unusual circumstances while in charter operation after Pan American had sold them in 1946. These two were destroyed at sea rather than salvaged. They were durable, serviceable machines and a good example of what could be expected of a modern counterpart in providing service to some of the undeveloped areas of Africa, South America and the Asian continent where extensive airport networks are not as commonplace as in North America and Europe.

The 314 wing was based on the Boeing B-15 design, which was bypassed by the US Army in favour of the B-17 Fortress of World War II fame. The first prototype aircraft was flown in June 1938, and after some changes in the vertical fin/rudder to improve directional stability the aircraft was put into production. The three vertical surfaces finally adopted remedied their directional problems. Initially, the six Model 314s were powered by 1600-hp engines. The second group of six, ordered by Pan American, had more powerful Double Cyclone engines and increased fuel capacity. Much of this fuel was carried in the sponsons. In flight, the 314s were comfortable in the extreme.

For a short time four of the 314s were inducted into the USAF, where they carried the military designation C-98. Following this short service, they were transferred to the US Navy and operated as part of the Contract Carrier programme under which they continued to be flown by civilian crews of Pan American.

Ranking even higher than the Short Sunderland as one of the all-time greats in the flying boat category is the Consolidated Model 28, PBY. The Model 28/PBY design was based on experience gained in the design and construction of the XPY flying boats which Consolidated had built for the US Navy beginning in 1929 and the XP3Ys which began their acceptance trials in March 1935. A period of developmental changes took place before an initial order for 60 P3Ys were ordered in June 1935. These P3Ys were powered by two 825-hp Pratt & Whitney R1830-54 engines. At about the same time the designation was changed to XPBY-1 (powered by 850-hp Pratt & Whitney

R-1830-64 engines), to reflect the expanded use of these aircraft as patrol/bombers rather than just the long-range patrol category. During this testing and modification period, one aircraft was sold as a civilian aircraft. Purchased by Dr Richard Archibald of the American Museum of Natural History for exploration work, this PBY-2 aircraft was christened the Guba. It saw service in this exploration capacity until it was sold to the USSR to carry out a search mission for Levanevsky, the famed Russian polar flyer.

On 14-15 October, 1935, Lieutenant Commander K McGinnis, Lieutenant J K Averill and a crew of four flew an XP3Y-1 from Cristobal Harbor, Canal Zone to Alameda, California in 34 hr 45 min, establishing two world records of 3281.3 miles (5280.7 km) straight-line distance and a total of 3443 miles (5540.9 km) overall distance. After assignments to squadrons, these aircraft began their operations and continued to set records. On

A Boeing 314 Clipper of Pan American Airways at anchor before the war. These aircraft were powered by four Wright Cyclone GR-2600 1700 hp engines and could carry 89 passengers. The Pan Am Clipper terminals included anchorages and luxury hotels for passenger stopovers. **During the war British Clippers were pressed into service as transports, but some remained to operate on restricted flights to Africa and India, while US Clippers skirted Japanese-held islands to link Australia and New Zealand with the USA**

21-22 June, 1937, 12 PBY-1s of Patrol Squadron 3 flew 3292 miles (5298 km) from San Diego to Coco Solo, Canal Zone in 27 hr 58 min.

The PBY Catalina in its many variants was produced in greater numbers than any other flying boat. They were produced in the US by Consolidated and the Naval Aircraft Factory; in Canada they were produced by Canadian Vickers (Canadair) and Boeing Aircraft of Canada, and they were also produced in the USSR under licence. In use the Model 28 (PBY) was almost as widely dispersed as the Douglas DC-3, serving in the military of the United States, Canada, the UK, Australia, New Zealand and the USSR during World War II and a host of other countries after the war. They were to see postwar service with airlines in all parts of the world and in private and commercial survey work as well. Numerically, it was to set a record for its type, with 3290 produced in the United States and Canada and an unknown number in the USSR.

During World War II they were called upon to do many things, some of which were previously thought to be impossible, including the rescue of downed airmen right under the guns of enemy antiaircraft batteries. Launching torpedoes, bombing and even modified dive bombing, were all included, though their usual routine was lone, often boring, patrols to search out submarines or provide early warning of enemy attack. Durability of the PBY is confirmed by the fact that they still exist in substantial numbers widely scattered throughout the world. An interesting aside is the fact that the PBY and the DC-3/C-47 were both powered by Pratt & Whitney R-1830 engines, some variants of which could be interchangeable.

In 1937, Grumman Aircraft Company designed a twin-engined amphibian which was ordered off-the-drawing-board by a number of private pilots and company executives. This was the Grumman G21 Goose, a handsome and efficient six/seven-place aircraft which proved to be popular in civil aviation and was acquired by the US Navy as utility category aircraft under the designation of JRF and by the US Army Air Corps as OA-9s. With the outbreak of World War II, the quantities on order were increased by both these services and a small order of three aircraft was added by the US Coast Guard. A number were delivered to the RAF as personnel transports and for air-sea rescue duties as Goose 1 and 1A. A number were also delivered to the RCAF and to the Portuguese navy. After the war, the French Aironavale used them for reconnaissance. They were all fitted for short-range reconnaissance duties but served mostly as staff transports and in other general utility duties. After the war most of the surviving G21s were acquired by civilian operators such as Antilles Air Boats in the Caribbean and a number of Canadian air services contractors. A number have been rebuilt incorporating more powerful reciprocating engines or, in more recent times, Pratt & Whitney PT-6 turboprop installation, and retractable wing-tip floats similar to those of the PBY. In each of these modifications the normal problem areas have been reworked. New cabin interiors have been fitted and the flight deck completely modernized in keeping with modern instrument flight and electronics requirements.

FLYING BOATS AT WAR

As war approached in Europe in 1938, several flying boat designs emerged, probably in anticipation of a military conflict. The first of these was the Blohm und Voss BV 138, whose geometry reverted back to the short hull/tail boom configuration of the Curtiss NC boats of World War I. The BV 138, however, was an all metal creation. It had a long gestation period and an equally long and difficult birth for it was completely redesigned at least once and various components had to be strengthened after tests. The hull was enlarged, the gull wing replaced by a straight wing, tail booms were strengthened and the cross-section changed from the original oval shape to a squared cross-section. Armament and its installation changed and the flaps and the vertical tail surfaces were enlarged. In this design, we see again the compromises that were required to keep the propellers and tail surfaces clear of the water spray generated by a high speed movement of a hull through rough water. The redesign eliminated the production and engineering problems involved with the gull-wing and the depth of the hull was increased and lengthened to preserve the proportions and increase the planing surface of the hull bottom.

The BV 138A-1 was first flown in April of 1940. In this version other structural weaknesses became apparent necessitating a return to the drawing board. The resulting BV 138 B-1, with improved armament, became the configuration to which all preceding production aircraft were modified. After all this redesign and modification, the aircraft were grounded during the winter of 1940-41 due to problems with the propellers and the Junkers Jumo 205C Diesel engines. For those not familiar with aircraft powerplants, it is worth relating that these engines were technically unique. They had six cylinders and 12 pistons. Two crankshafts at the upper and lower ends of the engine were geared to a common propeller shaft and two pistons operated in each cylinder timed to fire when the pistons converged at the centre of the cylinder. The Jumo 205s were the most successful and most produced of the very few diesel aircraft engine designs.

A serious shortage of waterborne aircraft during the Norwegian campaign, and the period immediately after its completion, kept the pressure on to push this aircraft through its problem period. They were pressed into service as transports, with a capacity of ten passengers, and in antishipping operations with bombers and submarines.

When all the developmental problems were behind them, the BV 138s proved to be very rugged aircraft. A few of the 138s were fitted with degaussing rings to be used in magnetic minesweeping duties.

An aircraft type that is often confused with the Short C Class flying boats was a successor, the Short S.26 G Class flying boat. Without a side-by-side size comparison it is easy to mistake the G Class aircraft. The G Class boats were larger in all dimensions but are easily mistaken due to the similarity of their geometry and profile. Two of the easiest identifying details are the two dorsal turrets and the knife edge second step on the G which is similar to that of the Sunderland. In all other respects they can be described as a stretched C Class aircraft.

Intended originally for transatlantic service, the first of three G Class boats, the Golden Hind, was first flown in

A Royal Navy Westland-
Sikorsky Dragonfly helicopter
passes the last Supermarine
Sea Otter in service in the
Mediterranean in 1953. The
aircraft are flying over Grand
Harbour, Malta. The helicopter's
ability to hover makes it an
ideal air-sea rescue aircraft

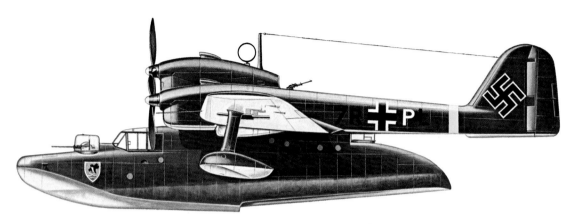

June, 1939. With the outbreak of the war they were immediately pressed into military service to serve as maritime reconnaissance aircraft. One aircraft was lost during military service due to an accident and the remaining two were turned over to BOAC in December, 1941, to be reconditioned for civil airline service. They continued to serve as high priority transports until the Golden Hind crashed in January 1943 due to an engine fire. Production was limited to the three examples in the works at the outbreak of the war. From then on the production capacity of the Short factory was devoted to Sunderland production and aircraft derivatives of the Sunderland. One of these derivatives, the Short S.25 Sunderland transport, designated the Hythe Class, was a made-over Sunderland.

Anticipating the cessation of hostilities, Short Brothers set to work to produce a completely civil transport version, the S.25 Sandringham, which appeared in 1945. All armament positions were neatly faired, producing a fine looking aircraft which would be ready at the end of the war. At the same time developments were under way on the Short Seaford, a more powerful and much heavier replacement for the Sunderland which would gross at 75 000 lb (34 000 kg), instead of the 65 000 lb (29 500 kg) of the Sunderland. Dimensionally the Seaford and Sunderland were almost identical, but the Seaford wings were strengthened and the powerplants were four 1800-hp Bristol Hercules 100s. As in the case of the Sandringham a civil variant was produced, for by 1945 the end of the war was in sight and it seemed prudent to have a plan in hand for conversion. This civil version was the Short S.45 Solent which made its debut in 1946, just in time for resumption of civil airline service. They proved to be very popular with passengers flying the Empire routes to South Africa until November 1950 when flying boat service ceased with the introduction of pressurized Handley Page Hermes landplanes which took over to continue the service.

In Germany, a trio of flying boats were being readied for war. These three aircraft types were all in the design and/or testing stage by one manufacturer. The Dornier 18 was basically a modernized Dornier Wal with its engines mounted in tandem on the centreline of the pylon-mounted monoplane wing. Originally intended to serve as a transatlantic mail carrier, the Do 18 made its debut just in time to be drafted into the Luftwaffe, though the first four delivered were civilian models for the Deutsche Lufthansa for service across the South Atlantic. An additional aircraft

BLOHM UND VOSS BV 138B-1

Known as the 'Flying Shoe' the BV 138 was a robust aircraft which operated throughout the war from Leningrad to the Atlantic

Span: 27.00 m (88 ft 7 in)	
Length: 19.85 m (65 ft 1½ in)	
Engine: 3 880 hp Junkers Jumo 205D 12-cylinder diesels	
Max speed: 275 km/h (171 mph)	
Max range: 4296 km (2670 miles)	
Armament: 2 20-mm cannon and 2 machine-guns with up to 300 kg (662 lb) of bombs or depth charges	

Bottom: A BOAC Short Solent lands on the Thames in May 1949 to mark the 30th anniversary of British commercial air transport. A second Solent can be seen in the top left corner.
Below: The Short Sandringham, a civilian version of the Sunderland V, skims the water as it takes off in 1945. The Sandringham had the bow and tail turrets faired over. They could carry up to 45 passengers in some comfort and remained in service up to 1966

The BOAC Speedbird Hythe class flying boat 'Huntingdon' on the river Nenam at Bangkok. This fairly crude conversion of a Sunderland III clearly shows the bow turret position. These aircraft began operating with Commonwealth and the British Overseas Airways Corporation as early as 1942 for mails and high priority passenger services. The first true 'Hythe' class aircraft, however, were postwar flying boats with higher rated Pegasus engines

Right: A Dornier Do 24 in prewar markings, the type was originally designed to a specification from the Dutch government. During the war it was built in the Netherlands and France and remained in service with the French after the Liberation

of the first production run, the Do 18F was fitted out for record breaking purposes. It had a stretched wing to establish a distance record of 5215 miles (8390 km) which was greater than the 4447-mile (7157-km) range of the Kawanishi H8K2 Emily. Part of the secret of this long-range flight lay with the choice of engines – Junkers 205C diesel engines which produced 700 hp each. Later the Do 18G had Jumo 205D engines of 880 hp. The Do 18 served in a number of roles, principally in military service during World War II as reconnaissance and air-sea rescue aircraft. It first entered service with the Luftwaffe in 1938 and continued in production, in a number of variants, until 1940 by which time slightly more than 100 Do 18s had been produced.

About the time that the Do 18 was being flight tested, another durable Dornier was in the design stage. This was the Do 24 which was designed for the Dutch government for use in the Dutch East Indies. It was a slightly larger aircraft than the Do 18, with a span of 88 ft 6 in (26.97 m) as opposed to the 77 ft 9 in (23.7 m) of the Do 18. The same general configuration of the Do 18 was followed, a high wing parasol monoplane with strut bracing between

the hull and wing and between the sponsons and the wing. The Do 24 was powered normally by three 1000-hp BMW Bramo Fafnir 323R-2 engines which gave good all round performance. As the war progressed, the Dutch Avialanda and de Schelde companies produced 25 of the Do 24s under licence before the Germans overran the Netherlands in 1940. Subsequently, production was resumed and a further 154 were produced in the Netherlands and another 48 were produced in France after the German occupation. Some of this latter group were operated by the French after the Allied liberation. Spain purchased a dozen of the transport model Do 24T for air-sea rescue duties. These remained in service until 1977. Some of the Do 24s were used by the Royal Australian Air Force, a number having escaped from the Japanese, and one single Do 24 was operated by the Swedish air force after it was interned. It was operated until 1951 when it was claimed as war booty by the USSR. In combat configuration, the Do 24 armament consisted of a 20-mm (0.787-in) MG 151 cannon in a dorsal turret and a single 7.9-mm (0.311-in) MG 15 machine-gun in the nose and tail. Ordnance was comparatively light, up to 12 110-lb (50-kg) bombs could

DORNIER Do 18

The Do 18 was originally designed to meet a requirement for a transatlantic mail carrier. Three prototypes were tested by Lufthansa who eventually operated a fleet of five aircraft. In its wartime role the Do 18 was fitted with two defensive turrets and a load of four light bombs

Span:	23.70 m (77 ft 9 in)
Length:	19.25 m (63 ft 1¾ in)
Engine:	2 600 hp Junkers Jumo 205C 6-cylinder diesels
Max speed:	265 km/h (165 mph)
Max range:	3500 km (2175 miles)
Armament:	1 13-mm machine-gun and later a 20-mm cannon in aft turret

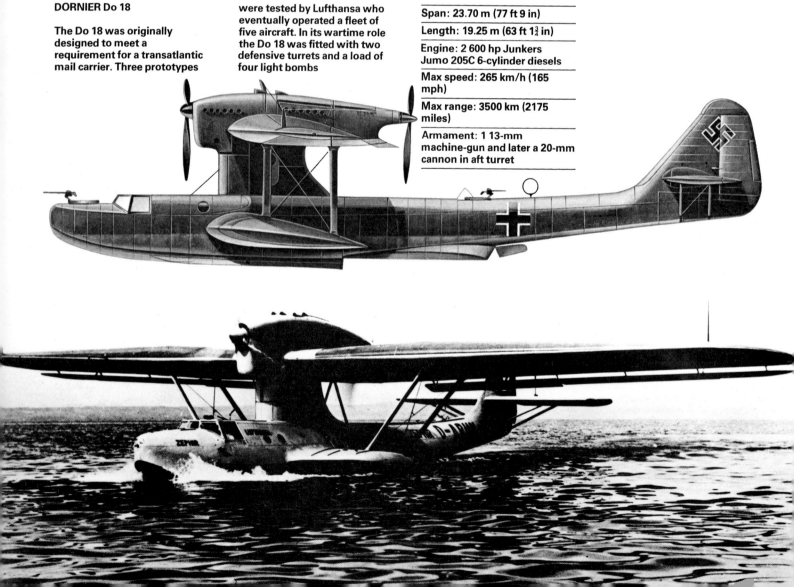

be carried under the wings. Cruising speed was a respectable 183 mph (295 km/h) and maximum range was almost 3000 miles (4800 km).

Another Dornier model originally developed for transatlantic mail service was the Do 26. A very clean design, it was powered by four Junkers Jumo 205C diesel engines of 700 hp each. An interesting technical feature of this aircraft was the installation of these liquid-cooled diesel engines, which were mounted in tandem at the break of the gull wing. To keep the propellers of the rear pusher engines out of the spray pattern, the rear engine thrust line was tilted upward 6° during take-off and landing. An added contribution to the clean design was the retractable wing-tip floats. Six Do 26s were built and were designed to be catapulted from merchant ships but their limited armament and limited passenger capacity reduced their service operations. It was one of the most attractive and technically interesting flying boats ever built. There was not to be another flying boat to rival it for cleanness of line until the design and construction of the Martin P6M Sea Master, a decade later. Unfortunately, their limited production and the date of their production almost guaranteed that no Do 26 would survive. Two were lost during the Norwegian campaign in May 1940 and the remaining aircraft were used in transport duties until the lack of spare parts decreed they would fly no more.

Due largely to the fact that the Do 26s were converted mail carriers, their armament was limited and ineffective. It consisted of a 20-mm cannon in an electrically operated bow turret, plus three 7.9-mm machine-guns mounted in two waist blisters and one in a waterproof hatch in the lower hull behind the rear of two steps.

About the same time as the Dornier flying boats were under development, Aeronautica Macchi of Varese, Italy, had in production a group of geometrically similar flying boats. These included a single-engined MC 77 monoplane flying boat, designed for long-range reconnaissance. It was an interesting, clean design constructed of wood. Plywood wings and hull resulted in an attractive design which could produce a good turn of speed, in excess of 180 mph (290 km/h) powered by a single engine. At about the same time, Aeronautica Macchi also produced a dual configuration aircraft which could be converted to either a flying boat or an amphibian. The Macchi C 94 construction was primarily wood, a material still favoured by a number of manufacturers even though their aircraft, when immersed in water for a period of time, increased in weight due to water absorption. This seemed to be a basic problem with wood aircraft in spite of efforts to prevent water retention. This characteristic made it necessary to beach these flying boats whenever possible, rather than let them float at anchor for prolonged periods as could be done with the metal hulled aircraft. The metal hulls brought their own set of problems however, with corrosion of rivets and other fittings.

The Macchi C 94 was a smaller aircraft than the PBY and, like the Rhorbach designs, mounted the wing directly on the top of the fuselage with the engines mounted well above the wing centre section. The wing span of the C 94 was 75 ft (22.86 m) as compared to the 104 ft (31.7 m) of the PBY. It could carry up to 12 passengers in either the amphibious or flying boat configuration. In the amphibian version, the wheels of the main gear were swung forward into streamlined pockets in the leading edge of the wing. A reconnaissance flying boat was also built along the same general lines as the C 94 but larger, with a wing span of 83 ft (25.3 m) and length of nearly 59 ft (18 m). The C 99 was powered by more powerful 836-hp Isotta-Fraschini 'Asso' liquid-cooled engines and mounted twin vertical fin/rudders directly in line with the two strut-mounted powerplants. Completing this quartet of contemporary flying boats was the C 100, a three-engined, commercial aircraft which had a span of 79 ft 10 in (24.3 m) and was powered by three 800-hp Alfa 126 RC 10 radial air-cooled engines mounted in strut-braced nacelles. All the aircraft of this

BLACKBURN B20

The unusual design of the B20 was intended to keep the propellers clear of the water at take-off and landing. In flight the planing bottom and wingtip floats retracted to give a streamlined fuselage

Span: 25.04 m (82 ft 2 in)	
Length: 21.22 m (69 ft 7½ in)	
Engine: 2 1720 hp Rolls-Royce Vulture 24-cylinder X type	
Max speed: 518 km/h (322 mph) without armament	

Estimated range: 2414 km (1500 miles) with armament

Armament: 8 machine-guns and 8 113-kg (250-lb) bombs

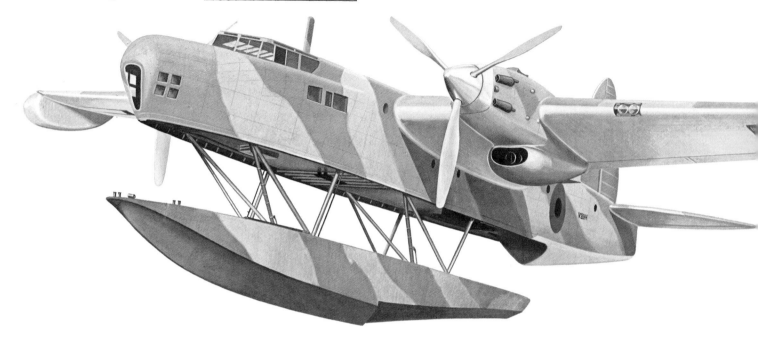

series had wire-braced, strut-mounted wing tip stabilizing floats mounted under the wings at the inboard end of the ailerons.

At this time in its aeronautical development, the USSR was quietly reducing its dependence on foreign manufacturers for the supply of aircraft. The Russians were still making purchases of one or two items of promising designs to examine and adopt foreign ideas to native-built aircraft then in design or production.

By 1938 design teams had been set up in the USSR to develop designs of standardized aircraft types. Out of these groups there evolved a comparatively modern and competitive design that was put into production as a successor to the Beriev MBR-2. This was a very modern design, the MDR-6 (naval long-range, reconnaissance) which was to replace the MDR-4. The MDR-6 was a twin-engined shoulder-wing aircraft, powered by two 1000-hp M-63 radial air-cooled engines mounted in well streamlined nacelles on top of the wing. It was an exceptionally clean design with a two-step hull and stabilizing floats at the mid-span position. It was capable of carrying bombs, torpedoes or depth charges on racks mounted under the wings. During the war the aircraft was further refined and 12-cylinder, liquid-cooled Klimov M-105A engines were installed for tests. In spite of the fact that they increased the weight of the MDR-6, they increased the speed by over 40 mph (64 km/h), and increased the operating ceiling of the MDR-6 which resulted in the MDR-6B. In Allied or NATO codenames these were known as the Madge and the Mug, respectively. The MDR-6, in its variations, was used throughout World War II from 1939 until 1944 by the USSR fleet units and was in service until the mid-1950s.

One of the most interesting and least successful flying boats of the early war period was the Saunders-Roe SARO Lerwick, a pudgy but nicely streamlined twin-engined, medium-range flying boat. The short two-step hull contributed to its lateral instability and did little for its appear-

ance. In profile it looks like a Sunderland which has been chopped off just behind the rear step. Most of its service career was devoted to testing and modification in a vain attempt to make the Lerwick an operationally acceptable aircraft. Though 20 aircraft were built, its service life was short and disastrous, for a number were lost during the testing and modification flight programme. Those that survived were scrapped or used for maintenance training.

In 1940 a new approach to flying boat design was launched by Blackburn Aircraft Ltd, combining features of flying boats and single-float hydroplanes on a large scale. The B.20 was a design in which the propellers were kept clear of the water while mounted on engines that were installed in the leading edge of the wing, providing a better aerodynamic combination. To accomplish this, the lower portion of the hull was constructed of a self-contained central float or hull. In flight, this float was tucked up against the fuselage producing a neat, low air resistance airframe. During take-off, landing and while at rest, this large central float was lowered simultaneously with the retractable wing-tip floats. This unusual design feature also placed the wing at its most advantageous angle of incidence for take-offs and landing. This was important because in a conventional design it is usually a compromise to place these closely related angles correctly and not interfere with the planing angle of the hull. The wing-tip floats, mounted on unbraced hydraulically operated struts retracted to form end plates at the wing tips of the cantilever wing in a manner similar to the floats on the Consolidated Mod 28 and 29, the Catalina and Coronado. It was an ingenious solution to a number of problems normally encountered in flying boat design. Its design was attributed, in patents, to Major JD Rennie, chief seaplane designer of Blackburn Aircraft Ltd. It was not a small aircraft, having a wing span of 82 ft (25 m) and a gross weight of 35 000 lb (15 875 kg).

The B.20 was powered by two supercharged Rolls-Royce Vulture, 24-cylinder, liquid-cooled engines whose

The first Blohm und Voss BV 222 Wiking prior to initial trials in the summer of 1940. The Wiking was the largest seaplane to attain production status in World War II. It had a crew of 11 to 14 and an operational range of 3400 km (2115 miles)

combined take-off power was 1720 hp. The wing was sheet metal construction and covered with fabric exterior skin on the flaps and ailerons. The first aircraft of the B.20 type was destroyed by accident. A second prototype under construction was discontinued due to the pressure of wartime demands which absorbed all design and factory production capacity.

With World War II under way a number of aircraft in development, which were anticipating such an eventuality began to emerge. Among these was the gigantic Blohm und Voss BV 222 Wiking. Making its first flight on 7 September, 1940, the prototype and sister aircraft were immediately impressed into service as Luftwaffe transports instead of service with Lufthansa, for whom the design was begun. Intended as a long-range transoceanic passenger transport for the North and South Atlantic services, the BV 222 was designed by a team headed by Dr Richard Vogt, one of Germany's foremost designers of flying boats.

As planned for Lufthansa, a large dining room and an eight-place cabin were available to the passengers in addition to a hallway over 20 ft (6 m) long. Four sleeping compartments held four beds each, each pair of beds being separated by a curtain.

An unusual feature of the BV 222 was the wing-tip floats. Each float was vertically divided with each half retracting, one rising inboard and one outboard to enable them to be housed within the depth of the wing. No cover plates were needed over the floats because the flat face of the half-float fitted flush with the lower surface of the wing. The floats were extended and retracted by a single motor located at the middle, in the fuselage behind the wing spars. All four float halves operated simultaneously and could also be operated manually through a hand crank which required 112 turns to raise or lower the floats. The gear ratio was chosen so that at 114.2 mph (183.8 km/h) the retraction time was about 15 sec. They had to be retracted before the air speed reached 140 mph (225 km/h).

In the early prototypes the power was insufficient for normal take-off. Therefore, the aircraft was fitted with four RATOG (rocket) units suspended under the wings to get the aircraft over the 'hump'. The units burned for 30 sec after which they were jettisoned at 500 ft by pulling release handles to allow the units to descend by parachute. Powerplants could be six of any of the following types:
   a) BMW 801, 14-cylinder, air-cooled, 2-row radial, with 1600 hp each
   b) BMW 802, 18-cylinder, air-cooled, 2-row radial, with 2050 hp each
   c) Junkers Jumo 211, 12-cylinder, inverted V, liquid-cooled, with 1400 hp each
   d) Junkers Jumo 207, 6-cylinder, opposed-piston, liquid-cooled diesel, with 1000 hp each

At just over 100 000 lb (45 350 kg), a wing span of 150 ft (45.7 m) and powered by six 1000-1400-hp engines which varied from one prototype to the next, the BV 222 was the largest German flying boat to be put into service during World War II, although a still larger BV 238 was being developed and built as a replacement. This BV 238 prototype was destroyed by Allied fighters while on the water.

Initially, the Wikings were unarmed. However, because of the nature of their mission, limited armament was fitted consisting of an MG 81 of 7.9-mm (0.311-in) which was fitted in the nose; two upper turrets each housing an MG 131 machine-gun of 13-mm (0.51-in) and four 7.9-mm MG 81s mounted in positions along the sides of the hull. At one point a pair of turrets were mounted atop the inboard portion of the wing but it was found that they disturbed the air flow and created unacceptable drag. As a result these were removed. Shortly after its test flights cargo doors were added to make it possible to carry oversize cargo, such as replacement engines for use by German aircraft during the Norwegian campaign and later supplying the Afrika Korps in Africa. During these supply missions several BV

HUGHES A-4 'SPRUCE GOOSE'

Originally conceived as a war-time answer to the U-boat threat the A-4 was intended to transport a cargo of up to 68 947 kg (152 000 lb)

Span: 97.69 m (320 ft 6 in)

Length: 66.6 m (218 ft 6 in)

Engines: 8 Pratt & Whitney R-4360 radials

Max speed: 350 km/h (218 mph)

Max range: 9495 km (5900 miles)

222s were lost over the Mediterranean when their fighter escort was destroyed or distracted by Allied fighters.

There is a parallel between Blohm und Voss of Hamburg and the Hughes-Kaiser efforts to produce an even larger aircraft – the Hughes-Kaiser HK-1 Hercules (also known as the Hughes H-4). Blohm und Voss, a shipbuilding firm of Hamburg, Germany, set up a subsidiary company to manufacture aircraft. Many of the aircraft produced by this company were waterborne types or derived from them, as in the case of the BV 139/142, the latter being a land-plane development of the former. In the United States, the shipbuilding firm headed by Henry J Kaiser decided to undertake construction of a giant flying boat to, in some way, parallel its shipbuilding mass-production efforts which were gaining much publicity during World War II. To design this monster aircraft, Kaiser formed a partnership with Howard Hughes who, in his own right, was wealthy beyond normal comprehension. The first obstacle to the design was the expected shortage of raw materials, if it was to be designed for metal construction. To preclude this possibility, the design was entirely of wood. The design team had to pioneer many areas of wood fabrication, many of which had utility in other fields of construction. The H-4 has had a generous share of publicity over the years, beginning with its construction and transport to a specially built assembly dock on the waterfront of Long Beach, California. The test flight of the Hercules on 2 November, 1947, piloted by Hughes, lifted out of the water to an altitude of about 70 ft (21 m) for something over a mile before returning to the water, never to rise again. Popularly known in the press as the 'Spruce Goose', this HK-1 or H-4 has over the years been the subject of much controversy during the Congressional hearings on its funding. There is also much speculation on its future especially during the times when the City of Long Beach has threatened to have it evicted from what has since become a choice waterfront commercial area.

The H-4's powerplants are Pratt & Whitney R4360 Wasp Major engines, known in the industry as 'Corncobs' because of the 28 air-cooled cylinders ranged in four staggered radial rows of seven cylinders each. They produced up to 3500 hp per engine and the HK-1 (H-4) has

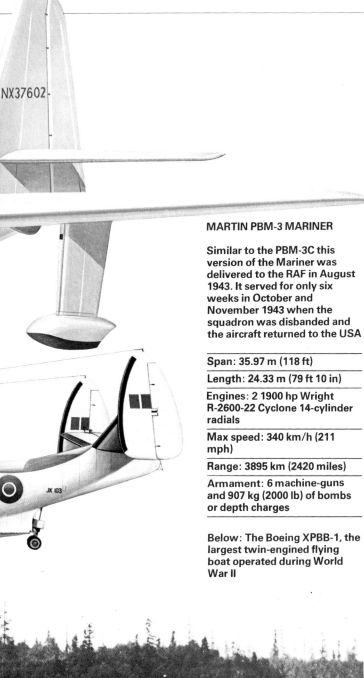

MARTIN PBM-3 MARINER

Similar to the PBM-3C this version of the Mariner was delivered to the RAF in August 1943. It served for only six weeks in October and November 1943 when the squadron was disbanded and the aircraft returned to the USA

Span: 35.97 m (118 ft)	
Length: 24.33 m (79 ft 10 in)	
Engines: 2 1900 hp Wright R-2600-22 Cyclone 14-cylinder radials	
Max speed: 340 km/h (211 mph)	
Range: 3895 km (2420 miles)	
Armament: 6 machine-guns and 907 kg (2000 lb) of bombs or depth charges	

Below: The Boeing XPBB-1, the largest twin-engined flying boat operated during World War II

eight of these engines mounted in nacelles along the leading edge of the wing. Large as these engines and their nacelles are, they are dwarfed by the gigantic wing itself making them appear to be slender fingers extending forward from the leading edge. It was designed to carry as many as 750 passengers or about 350 stretcher-borne hospital patients. Alternatively, it could carry up to 35 tons of cargo for limited range. While the press derisively called the H-4 the Spruce Goose, it is, in fact, built of birch plywood with small amounts of spruce used as fillers.

A contemporary of the Consolidated PBY was the Martin PBM-Mariner. One of the interesting aspects of the design and production of the Martin Model 162 (PBM) was the construction of a so-called quarter-scale model to test the aerodynamic and hydrodynamic characteristics of the Mariner. The model, if you can call it that, is a single-seat, single-engined aircraft powered by a Pobjoy engine. The model, known as the Model 162A, still exists in the National Aircraft Collection of the Smithsonian.

The full-size prototype of the Mariner, the XPBM-1, flew in 1939. Like the PBY, the Mariner was a twin-engined machine but that is where similarities end. It was a much larger aircraft, powered by Wright R-2600-6 engines of 1600 hp for take-off. To accommodate the large diameter propellers, the wings were designed in a gull-shape to place the wing-mounted engines well clear of the spray pattern. The first group of 20 PBM-1s had another distinguishing feature. The wing floats were retractable. Later models had fixed wing-tip floats. The horizontal stabilizer had a dihedral that matched the angle of the gull wing and a pair of fin/rudders which were attached at right angles to the stabilizer, resulting in an easily recognized pigeon-toed or converging appearance of the empennage. The aircraft was developed to the PBM-3, which entailed the change to more powerful R-2600-12 engines and replacing the retractable floats with fixed wing-tip floats. The first 50 of this revised model were fitted as transports with reinforced cargo floors. They were designated PBM-3Rs and were delivered to the Naval Air Transport Service.

In the combat configuration the PBM-3s had increased fuel capacity and in the PBM-3Cs and 3D variants had uprated R2600-22 engines of 1900 hp each. A dorsal search radar was mounted just behind the flight deck. A bomb load of 8000 lb (3630 kg) was carried in the extended engine nacelles, and power-operated turrets in the nose and dorsal gun positions completed the combat load.

A still more powerful variant was tested – the PBM-5, for which orders were placed for 1000 units. The end of hostilities at VJ Day resulted in the cancellation of all aircraft not actually in production. Still, almost 600 of the PBM-5s were produced. After VJ, the Mariners were used for air-sea warfare patrols and a number were used by the US Coast Guard for air-sea rescue duties. In the final stages of production, 36 PBM-5As were produced with retractable tricycle landing gear and more powerful R-2600-34 engines, making this the largest amphibian built to this date. Total wartime production of the Mariner was 1289 aircraft. A small number, about 25, were operated by the RAF under lend-lease provisions.

Another Martin aircraft under development prior to the war was the Model 170 XPB2M-1 Mars, later redesignated

US Navy Martin Mars transports which operated after World War II. When they retired from service Fairey Aviation of Canada converted them into water bombers capable of carrying 26 500 litres (7000 gallons) for fire fighting

JRM-1. As a prewar design, provisions for combat service based on experience gained as the war progressed, were not readily incorporated in the PB2M-1 other than power-operated gun turrets in the nose and tail. Since conversion of the Mars to full combat capability would have been prohibitively expensive the aircraft was converted to a transport version. In this configuration the designation was changed to XPB2M-1R and the aircraft assigned to NATS, after which it began to set records. On its first flight in December 1943, the Mars carried a 13 000-lb (5900-kg) load from Patuxent Naval Air Station, Maryland, to Natal, Brazil, a distance of 4375 miles (7040 km) non-stop. This was followed in early 1944 by a flight to Hawaii, a distance of 4700 miles (7560 km), with a payload of 20 500 lb (9300 kg). A much modified version, designated JRM-1, was ordered in January 1945, but only five of the 20 aircraft ordered were in production before hostilities ceased. In this version the hull was modified and a single vertical fin/rudder replaced the twin rudders of the PB2M-1. It was powered by four 2300-hp Wright R-3350-8 engines. Gross weight was 145 000 lb (65 770 kg) and the wing span was 200 ft (61 m), approaching the size of the much publicized Hughes (HK-1) Hercules. Hopes for commercial passenger models were short lived but development continued with three additional aircraft, the last of which was delivered in mid-1946. In May 1946, the Marshall Mars established an unofficial record carrying 301 passengers and a crew of seven from Alameda Naval Air Station to San Diego Naval Air Station. The final Mars, designated JRM-2, was delivered in late 1947. Its operating gross weight was 165 000 lb (74 850 kg). After retirement from service, four Mars aircraft were purchased by Flying Tankers Ltd of Canada. They were modified as water bombers for fire-fighting duties where they are still used. In fighting fires they are capable of scooping up 7000 gal of water into internal fibreglass tanks during one pass over the surface of a lake. Water is taken aboard by scoops projecting below the hull. They are still operating as required by their new duties and could serve as test beds for new flying-boat developments including the installation of turboprop engines or, possibly, nuclear powerplants.

A scaled-down version of the Grumman G-21 Goose was the G-44 Widgeon which was first flown in July 1940. Like the Goose, the Widgeon was intended as a private aircraft but was drafted into military service like so many of their contemporaries. At least three or four were allocated to Pan American Airways as crew trainers and were stationed at the New York Marine Terminal. The majority of those produced were given the naval designation of J4F-1 and were used for inshore submarine patrol or as trainers. They were powered by 200-hp air-cooled Ranger engines and were capable of carrying a crew of two and a single 200-lb (90.7-kg) depth charge. An original order of 25 was placed by the US Navy for service with the US Coast Guard. The US Air Force placed an order for 16 which were delivered in 1942 and designated OA-14. Another 15 aircraft were ordered for delivery to the RAF under lend-lease and were operated as Gosling Is in the West Indies during 1943-45. After the war about 50 aircraft were produced as civil/private aircraft and a number of military surplus aircraft were converted back to civilian specifications to be used as executive aircraft and by the US Fish and Wildlife Service. A number were further modified by changing engines, from the inverted in-line air-cooled Rangers to 6-cylinder, horizontally-opposed air-cooled 270-hp Lycoming GO-480 engines and were known as McKinnon Super Widgeons. About 40 Widgeons built under licence by Société de Constructions Aero-Navales in France were also sold in the United States, many of which were converted by installing 300-hp Lycoming R-680 radial, air-cooled engines and remanufacturing the airframes. Many are still operating at this late date, some 38 years after the first Widgeon was test flown.

An interesting application of hydrodynamic testing procedures was engineered to use a Widgeon as the test vehicle. When the design of the Martin P5M-1 Marlin was being developed, a means of testing the long-afterbody hull design was required. To determine the best of three alternative hull forms, a Widgeon was converted to accept the three hulls interchangeably so that actual operating conditions could be the basis of the choice rather than 'guesstimates' or tank testing exclusively. The test vehicle was duly designated XP5M-1. To make this jack-of-all-trades, an angle contour extrusion was riveted to the exterior of the Widgeon hull above the water line, completely around the hull beltline, then the lower hull plating and frames were cut away flush with this angle extrusion. Three different hull bottoms were then manufactured and,

SUPERMARINE SEA OTTER

The Sea Otter was intended to replace the Walrus, but though it first flew in 1938 it was not until November 1944 that it entered service. Bottom: A Supermarine Sea Otter throttles back as it comes in to land

Span: 14 m (46 ft)	
Length: 11.8 m (39 ft 2 in)	
Engine: 1 855 hp Bristol Mercury XXX 9-cylinder radial	
Max speed: 241 km/h (150 mph)	
Max range: 1166 km (725 miles)	

SHORT SHETLAND

Right: The Short Shetland as a postwar civil transport with accommodation for 40 passengers. In this guise it first flew in 1947 at Rochester, Kent. **Below:** The Shetland during the war when it was intended to be a long-range reconnaissance flying boat.

Span: 45 m (150 ft 4 in)	
Length: 33 m (110 ft)	
Engine: 4 2500 hp Bristol Centaurus XI 18-cylinder radials	
Max speed: 423 km/h (263 mph)	
Max range: 6957 km (4323 miles)	

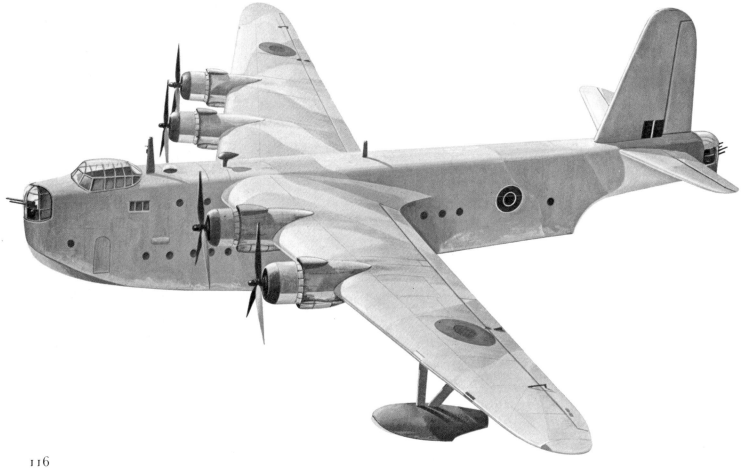

one at a time, bolted by means of an adjacent facing angle to the upper part of the hull to be used for a 'fly-off' test. By this method, the final configuration of the hull bottom was determined. The only negative aspect of this procedure was the number of bolts that had to be loosened and tightened with each change. With a spacing of about 3 in (76.2 mm), there were a few hundred bolts for the test mechanics to remove and replace. This aircraft, with modified hull and modified landing gear retraction system, is still in existence.

The Supermarine type 309 Sea Otter was designed as a replacement for the war-weary Walrus which had been carrying the load and was badly in need of improvement. The Otter became available in 1944. It had the same general appearance as the Walrus but the powerplant installation was changed from a pusher configuration on the Walrus to a tractor installation. Like the Walrus, the Otter was designed to operate from carriers and served primarily as an air-sea rescue aircraft but was also fitted to carry bombs or depth charges on universal racks under the lower wings. While like the Walrus in many ways, the Otter was a much improved machine aerodynamically, more streamlined and more powerful, being fitted with an 855-hp Bristol Mercury XXX air-cooled radial instead of a 775-hp Bristol Pegasus VI air-cooled radial. This combination gave the Otter about a 25 mph (40 km/h) advantage over the Walrus, a substantial increase when they both flew at less than 150 mph (240 km/h). The Walrus had reached 740 units by the end of its production while the Otter had only 290 completed machines, production being halted with the end of hostilities in sight.

The Short Shetland was a British flying boat designed to be about the same weight class as the German Blohm und Voss 222 discussed earlier. Production of the Sunderland and its variants occupied Short's design and production staff so that the Shetland came along about five years later than the BV 222 and was a direct contemporary of the successor BV 238 which had a designed gross weight of only 1 ton less. There are other similarities between the Shetland and the BV 238 including their general appearance. The BV 238 was slightly larger dimensionally and in wing area and had marginally greater power with six Daimler-Benz DB603V 12-cylinder inverted-V, liquid-cooled engines of 1750-hp each compared to the Shetland which was powered by four Bristol Centaurus XI 18-cylinder air-cooled radial engines of 2500 hp each.

The Shetland prototype was produced as a long-range reconnaissance aircraft. It was lost on 28 January, 1946 as a result of a fire while it was moored. A second Shetland prototype was completed but, due to the late date of its completion in mid-1947, it was completed as a civil airline configuration. While a few test flights were made it was evident that, as a civil airline transport, the sands of time were running out for flying boats and the Shetland did not offer any great improvement over existing types to warrant its retention and development. It was, therefore, scrapped.

It should be added here that the BV 238 did not survive the war either, for the single prototype was caught at its moorings by a flight of P51 Mustangs on the prowl for targets of opportunity. It proved to be a big target and one likely to fill the sights of the gun cameras as they straffed it to destruction.

DREAMS AND DESIGNS

The end of World War II did not bring flying boat production to a complete halt, as a number of aircraft still in the design stage moved forward to replace earlier designs from which so much had been learned in long and arduous service. While the momentum was still present a number of designs continued to emerge.

One of the most interesting of these immediate postwar designs was the Saunders-Roe SARO SR A1, a flying boat fighter developed to serve in forward combat areas in bays, lakes and rivers. As a concept it could be related to the Nakajima A6M2-N Rufe and the Kawanishi N1K1 Rex. Both these earlier types and the SR A1 were designed to provide fighter cover at forward areas until air strips could be constructed on islands.

The Rufe was a makeshift development of the Type O or Zeke, while the Rex was originally designed as a float-type fighter which was later developed into a land-based fighter, codenamed George.

A lesser known flying boat design along similar lines and approximately equal size was the Parnall Prawn of 1930 vintage. Like the SR A1 it was a single-seat military flying boat powered by a very modest 65 hp AC-Ricardo-Burt engine. In flight the engine thrust line of the Prawn was in horizontal position along the line of the fuselage. During take-off and landing the engine, and its tiny 4-ft (1.2-m) propeller, designed as a power package, were tilted upward at about a 20° angle to provide a deflected thrust and also to keep the propeller clear of the spray. The same idea was later used on the Dornier Do 26 flying boats but with pusher engines.

The SARO SR A1 was unique for, not only was it a flying boat fighter, but it was also a jet-powered aircraft. Theoretically, this was an ideal design because the fuselage and hull were the same, not forced to suspend a float on struts far enough to permit the propeller to be out of the spray pattern. During take-off a huge spray pattern was all that was visible as the jet engine developed its initial thrust. It should be remembered that the early turbo-jet engines were slow to accelerate the airframe, therefore the SR A1 was a very logical step. The water operations usually enjoyed the luxury of long, smooth take-off areas where the land-based aircraft required extra runways or special design features to improve the short-field take-off capability.

Like the Japanese fighter floatplanes, the SR A1 was designed during the war for the same type of service and for operations in the Pacific theatre. It was a relatively large aircraft, powered by two Metropolitan-Vickers (Metrovick) F 2/4 Beryl turbo-jet engines of 3850 lb (1746 kg) thrust each of which were mounted side-by-side in the fuselage with their jet pipes angled outward about 5° to clear the rear part of the hull and the tail surfaces. The air intake was through a single nose intake which was fitted with a scoop for use during take-off and landing operations to prevent ingestion of sea water into the engines.

Three prototype aircraft were built and tested, followed by a programme of demonstrations for the military and at the SBAC Show at Farnborough in September 1947. In spite of spectacular performance no serious interest developed, further evidence that the fortunes of the flying boat were on the decline and little help could be expected.

A CL-215 amphibian of the
French Protection Civile
operating in the South of
France as a water bomber.
Water bombers play an
important part in fighting the
forest fires that devastate the
woodland of the Cote d'Azur

SAUNDERS-ROE SR/A1

The world's first jet-powered flying boat to fly, the SR/A1 made its maiden flight at Cowes on 15 July 1947.

Span:	14.02 m (46 ft)
Length:	15.24 m (50 ft)
Engine: 1 1474 kg (3250 lb) st Metropolitan-Vickers F2/4 Beryl MVB 1 turbojet	
Max speed: 824 km/h (512 mph)	
Armament: (proposed) 4 20-mm Hispano cannon	

Regrettably, two of the three prototypes were scrapped. The one remaining example retained by the RAF is now exhibited at the Skyfame Museum in Gloucestershire. It is one of the most handsome flying boats ever to be designed and the concept might still be resurrected to meet a similar requirement in the future.

A contemporary of the SARO SR A1 was a less attractive but more utilitarian amphibian, the Grumman G-64/SA-16 Albatros. In nautical terms, the Albatross is one of the less popular birds, but in aircraft the Albatros is usually a most welcome sight. It was designed as a multipurpose aircraft for the US Navy but in its utility and air-sea rescue duties it found ready acceptance by the US Air Force and a number of foreign air services. It is a very robust and seaworthy aircraft which, only now, is being phased out of service. Those aircraft that have been declared surplus find ready demand though they have not been certificated for civil transport duties. Conversion of the Albatros to turbo-prop powerplants is one of several projects being actively promoted and engineered. It is known, from many demonstrations under adverse conditions, that the Albatros is worthy of the cost of making the conversion to civil certification standards. Designed from the beginning to have amphibious capacity, it was successfully tested as a triphibian by a retrofitted kit which also enabled it to land on snow. The kit consisted of skis attached to the keel and floats. Since the engineering and testing of a 'civilianized' version is still pending at this time, the passenger capacity is not known, but its present gross weight approached 30 000 lb (13 608 kg) and a turboprop installation will surely permit a higher gross weight limitation.

Earlier in the text we mentioned the conversion of a Grumman Widgeon into a test vehicle for the Martin P5M Marlin. It was designated, in its new form, the XP5M 'Petulant Porpoise' though it resembled the Marlin in only one respect, the design of the hull bottom which had a length-to-beam ratio of approximately 8.5:1. The Marlin Project began in mid-1946 but due to the extensive test programme related to the hull design, it was mid-1950 before production of the P5M was authorized by contract. It was designed as a replacement for the P4M Mariner and was produced until the end of 1960 in a number of variants.

The first aircraft of the series had the stabilizer mounted at the base of the vertical fin but as the series continued in production, the advantages of a T tail design were being explored in the NACA test wind tunnels and the results applied to a number of aircraft under design. The Marlin was one of these aircraft and was designated the P5M-2 when it was produced in 1953. A prominent, blister-shaped flight deck extended above the straight line of the top of the fuselage and its bulbous radar dome nose reminds one of the Jeep Cartoon of World War II or, possibly even W C Fields. Two Wright R-3350 Cyclone engines of 3450 hp each turned four-blade propellers. Extensions of the engine nacelles, under the wind, provided bays for the carrying of depth charges, torpedoes, or other categories of ordnance as required, up to 8000 lb (3630 kg) maximum. It could also carry another 8000 lb on external racks under the wings. Maximum speed of the Marlin was almost 250 mph (402 km/h) making it one of the fastest flying boats. The aerodynamically clean configuration of the aircraft also made one of the most attractive boats. Lessons learned in its design were to show up later in the Martin P6M Seamaster. The P5M remained in operation until 1966 serving with the US Coast Guard and the US Navy.

An aircraft that experienced a troubled history almost rivalling that of the Hughes H-4 (HK-1) was the Saunders-Roe SR-45 Princess which was designed from the beginning as a civilian airline transport. Rumours circulated at one time that it was seriously considered as a vehicle for testing a nuclear aircraft powerplant, a subject which has blown hot and cold on several occasions. The Princess was smaller than the Hughes aircraft, but that is not a fair comparison for the Princess had a most impressive wing span of 210 ft 6 in (64.2 m). With its massive three-level hull, the monoplane wing was, because of the propellers, mounted as a shoulder-level installation at the top of the fuselage.

Externally the Princess appears to be powered by six engines, there being six well-streamlined nacelles mounted in the leading edge of the wing. However, pairs of coupled engines were installed in each of the four inboard nacelles. The Princess was designed to be powered by Rolls-Royce Tweed turboprop engines. Delays in the development of these engines resulted in their replacement by Bristol Proteus Series 600 turboprops.

The hull was designed as a 'double bubble' which, in cross-section, was like a figure eight squeezed flat at the juncture of the two circles. Below this was appended a hull which made use of the most advanced hydrodynamics of

GRUMMAN SA-16 ALBATROS

The Albatros first flew in 1947 and was intended to be a utility amphibian. It has a crew of five or six and can carry up to 22 passengers.

Span: 29.46 m (96 ft 8 in)

Length: 19.18 m (62 ft 10 in)

Engine: 2 1425 hp Wright R-1820-76A radials

Max speed: 379 km/h (236 mph)

Max range: 4587 km (2850 miles)

Armament: (ASW role) 4 Mk 43 torpedoes or 2 Mk 43 torpedoes and 2 Mk 54-2 or Mk 101 depth charges

Left: A Grumman Albatros taxies up a coastal hard in the United States. The Albatros has been exported to 12 nations through the MAP programme and Norway and Spain operate ASW versions

MARTIN MARLIN P-5

A postwar design, the Marlin first flew in May 1948. The distinctive 'nose' houses an APS-80 radar and there are twin 20-mm cannon in the sting position. Normal crew strength is 8

Span: 36.02 m (118 ft 2 in)

Length: 30.66 m (100 ft 7 in)

Engine: 2 3250 hp Wright R-3350-30WA Turbo-Compounds

Max speed: 402 km/h (250 mph)

Range: 4634 km (2880 miles)

Armament: 8 450-kg (1000-lb) bombs and 2 910-kg (2000-lb) bombs

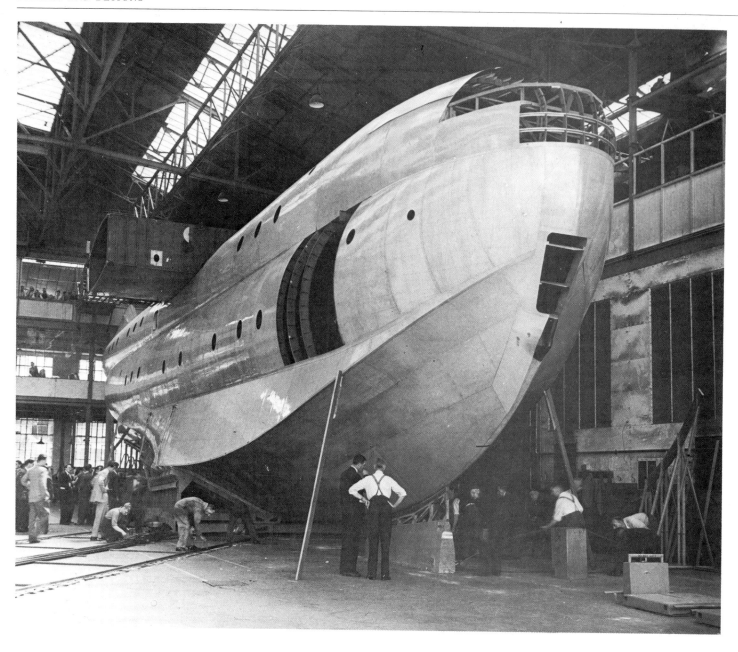

the long-afterbody. The 'double bubble' design was similar to that of the Curtiss CW-20 or C-46 Commando and the Boeing 377 Stratoliner. In the Princess it was to make provision for the cabin pressurization system, as was the case in the Stratoliner. It was the first time that pressurization was applied to a flying boat design. The 'bubbles' and their structural joint divided the hull into two decks for seating over 100 passengers.

The Princess was turned down by BOAC as an airline service type, whereupon the Ministry of Supply directed that they be turned over to the RAF to be tested for conversion to a long-range reconnaissance aircraft. The three Princesses became a highly political subject totally aside from their technical merits. The almost total conversion to land-planes left no room in BOAC's fleet for anything so massive or operationally unacceptable as a Princess. The RAF also found itself in a similar predicament for, by this time, operational funding was severely restricted in a postwar economy and the last thing they wanted was an orphan of any kind much less one of such huge dimensions which would require special handling and funding.

The times were not right for such an aircraft. The second and third Princesses were never completed but were mothballed for a number of years at Calshot until more powerful engines were developed, or until the political furore died down. The first Princess, registered G-ALUN, was tested for a time and even made a dramatic appearance at the 1952 Farnborough show. While preparing for the installation of more powerful engines, it was discovered that the gear boxes for the coupled engines would require complete redesign. This was an expense that was not justified in view of the lack of enthusiasm for the aircraft. After a testing programme, the prototype was also cocooned in 1954 joining its sister ships at Calshot. Eventually, all three were disposed of after the project and its costs were long forgotten or overtaken by inflation making them diminish in magnitude.

During the 1950s, the turboprop powerplant was still a very important form of propulsion in the UK, USSR and the US. As a consequence, a number of aircraft were under development in each of these countries to use this form of propulsion. The Princess and the Vickers Viscount are two examples. In the United States the Lockheed Electra II is probably the best known example due to the tragic events surrounding its introduction into airline service. A little-known flying boat was also being developed to be powered by a turboprop engine. This was the Convair R3Y

Left: The impressive hull of a
Saunders-Roe Princess under
construction at Cowes, Isle of
Wight.
Below: A Convair Tradewind
disgorges an artillery tractor
and howitzer from its belly hold
during trials in the late 1950s

Tradewind, which could have been Convair's ticket back to leadership in the aircraft production world. Instead, after a very careful programme of design, development and testing, the R3Y Tradewind is comparatively unknown except by those insiders who follow the trials and tribulations of the industry. The Tradewind was the only turbo-prop-powered flying boat to be accepted by the US Navy. It was designed to serve as a patrol boat but was converted to a transport. The first of these was flown in April, 1950 after a test programme that was very thorough and included such insurance features as use of the first dynamic test model to be flown by radio controls. It was a further refinement of the practice of working out design details by using 'models'. The same idea was used in the case of the Saunders-Roe Shrimp which was used to test technical details of the Saunders-Roe Princess and the Martin 162.A which pre-tested features of the Martin P4M Mariner. Both of these 'model' aircraft were built to a scale large enough to be flown by human pilots. The end purpose of each of the 'models' was to test with a minimum risk, both financial and human, the desired features of a proposed design.

By the time the R3Y was under development radio-controlled models were more reliable. Improvements in

the miniature engine field and improvements in radio control resulted from World War II experiments with radio-controlled drones and glide bombs. A further extension of these developments is the great current emphasis in RPVs (remote piloted vehicles).

The Tradewind was a ruggedly handsome high-wing monoplane powered by Allison XT-40-A-4 engines which were themselves an interesting development. They were in fact two turbine engines mounted side-by-side to a single gearbox to drive a single propeller shaft which delivered 5850 shp per paired, coupled engine.

The flight deck of the Tradewind protruded above the upper line of the fuselage, in much the same way as on the Boeing 747s, in order to give an unobstructed fuselage interior. This clear fuselage interior made it possible to load, straight-in, large military vehicles and standard cargo containers. This made it possible to deliver cargo or vehicles, straight from the dock, into the fuselage through a massive bow door and, on arrival at destination, they could reverse the loading procedure to deliver cargo straight onto a dock or beachhead. It was an airborne version of the well-known LSTs of World War II. The R3Y-1 had a long hull, almost 140 ft (42.67 m) long, a wing span of 145 ft 9 in (44.42 m) and a gross weight of 160 000

**The Convair XF2Y-1 Sea Dart
deploys its hydro-skis during
trials on San Diego Bay,
California. The Sea Dart
became the first flying boat to
pass the Mach 1 barrier**

lb (72 575 kg). It was a fast aircraft with a cruising speed of
300 mph (480 km/h). It would be an ideal starting point for
development of a modern-day fleet of flying boats to enter
cargo airline service to undeveloped areas of the globe.

An interesting replay of the waterborne fighter concept
had a short life in a design by Convair – the XF2Y-1 Sea
Dart. It was technologically another step along the way
from the Saunders-Roe SR/A-1 but, like the SR/A-1, it too
faced an uphill battle. The technical features could be
applied to larger aircraft but so far they had not re-
appeared. The Sea Dart incorporated such niceties as a
delta wing, which, because of its location, also provided
lateral stability when on the water, there being no requirement for wing-tip floats in the accepted form. It had a boat
hull, two Westinghouse J-34 turbojet engines and last, but
by no means least, retractable hydro-skis were fitted. The
first XF2Y-1 made its first flight on 9 April, 1953, rising out
of the water on a pair of skis, not unlike a water skier. The
test programme verified the technical possibilities of this
aircraft configuration and succeeded in pushing a flying
boat beyond Mach 1. This was on 3 August, 1954, before
disaster struck in the form of a mid-air disintegration of
one of the aircraft. The second aircraft is retained for
future study in the collection of the National Air and Space
Museum of the Smithsonian Institution.

The Martin P6M Seamaster prototype, which made its
first test flight on 14 July 1955, embodied all the design
features developed during World War II and immediately
after the war. In 1952 Martin was awarded a contract, first,
for a design study, and then a production contract for two
prototypes known as Model 275. They would be modern in
almost every way if produced today, several years after

their untimely destruction during tests. They were effectively seagoing B-52s, having a small crew of four and a
gross take-off weight of 160 000 lb (72 575 kg), the same as
the Tradewind. The technology involved in its design was
the latest known and included four Pratt & Whitney J75-P-
2 turbojet engines of 17 500 lb (7938 kg) thrust mounted
on top of a highly swept shoulder-mounted drooped wing
which had a span of 100 ft (30.5 m). It had a T tail
configuration and a high length-to-beam ratio of its 134 ft
(41 m) hull. The engines were mounted in such a way as to
prevent ingestion of the water spray pattern into the
engine air-intake ducts and the wing-tip floats were integ-
ral, enlarged parts of the drooped wing configuration.
These floats served additionally as wing-tip plates and in
the mooring and docking of the Seamaster they played an
important role in picking up the mooring buoy which was
the key to swinging the aircraft, almost automatically, into
the floating beaching gear or into a dock, whichever system
was being used at the time. Also incorporated in the design
of the P6Ms was a watertight rotary bomb bay. This could
be flipped over in flight to expose the bomb racks which
could be loaded on the inside of the hull with bombs,
mines, cameras or other ordnance stores. Unfortunately,
both XP6M-1s crashed during testing and only one YP6M-
1 and three P6M-2s were produced out of a total combined
order of 30 aircraft. They and the Seamaster project were
terminated in the autumn of 1959.

The flying boats now being designed in Japan for civilian
transportation bear a striking resemblance to these interesting Seamasters. They were well advanced technologically and though they experienced difficulties during their
test phase, history abounds with examples of greater loss as

The Martin **P6M-2 Seamaster** was powered by four 7938 kg (17 500 lb) st Pratt & Whitney J75-P-2 turbojets. It had a rotary bomb door which gave a water-tight protection to a pay-load of bombs, mines or cameras. The tactical concept behind the Seamaster was that it could operate in small numbers and be refuelled and rearmed by submarines or other small naval craft. In this way there would be no obvious carrier or airfield as a home base for enemy bomber or missile attacks

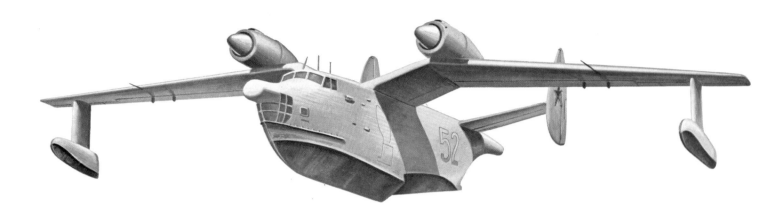

well as greater perseverance and final and rewarding success.

The flying boat or amphibian provides an ideal solution to the transport problems caused by the huge undeveloped land mass of the USSR. As many in the industry know, the Russian designers have made greater use of turboprops. They have not been in any great hurry to rush through this phase of aircraft powerplant utilization before it has been fully developed and exploited. A good example is the Beriev Be 12. Designed to fill the same role as the earlier Beriev Be-4 and the Be-6 Madge, the Be 12, known as the Mail by NATO, is a thoroughly modern long-range patrol plane with what appears to be the latest in sea-going detection and antishipping hardware. Their first public display was at Tushino in 1961 and after that they went on to amass a very impressive series of international records for flying boats in the categories of height, payload and speed. The design of the Be 12 is somewhat unorthodox by western standards but it is hard to fault success. The Be 12 is a twin-engined gull-wing monoplane amphibian resembling a goose with outstretched wings. The twin fins and rudders trail directly behind a pair of 4000 hp Ivchenko AI-20D turboprop engines. The gross take-off weight of the Mail is about twice the weight of the Grumman Albatros but with more than twice the horse-power – a very fine combination from a pilot's point of view. As amphibians go it is a very efficient machine which will remain in service for some years.

For singleness of purpose in the design the Canadian-built Canadair CL-215 is a prime example which became operational in 1969. From the outset, the CL-215 was designed for use in patrolling the vast forest areas of Canada and, when required, to be able to muster effective and fast response to forest fires. Usually a fast response will enable the fire fighters to contain and extinguish a forest fire before it has an opportunity to gain ground. In addition to its proven ability as a 'water bomber', the CL-215 can carry up to 19 passengers, primarily fire fighters, and equipment to the scene of a fire. The abundance of lakes throughout Canada makes it possible to move fire crews and their equipment within reasonable operating distance from fires, many of which are kindled by lightning strikes during storms.

The very angular structural parts of the CL-215 would appear to lend themselves to economical production and to

BERIEV BE-12 TCHAIKA (SEAGULL)

NATO code name Mail, the Be-12 was first seen at the Tushino air display in 1961. The Be-12 has a readily recognisable profile with its gull-wing layout, twin tail and the MAD (Magnetic Anomaly Detector) in the extreme rear fuselage.

Span: 30m (98 ft 5 in)	
Length: 30 m (98 ft 5 in)	
Engine: 2 4000 shp Ivchenko AI-20D turboprops	
Max speed: 608 km/h (378 mph)	
Max range: 4000 km (2485 miles)	
Armament: not known	

easy maintenance in the field. A tribute to their design is the fact that the type is also used by the French Department of Civil Protection along the French Riviera. This is a tangible acknowledgement that it is good for the job it was designed to do.

The most recent flying-boat design to reach production is the Japanese designed and built Shin Meiwa PS-1 (patrol sea-1) which was designed for the Japanese Maritime Self-Defence Force in 1972 and entered service in February, 1975.

Its design incorporates in a very efficient form all the latest technological innovations. As originally produced, it was a flying boat but with the addition of retractable landing gear the aircraft type was redesignated US-1. They can take off and land in very rough seas, having done so in waves as high as 4 m (13 ft), making them operational in Pacific waters 86% of the time. The US-1 is essentially an air-sea rescue aircraft designed to replace the Grumman Albatros which served with the JMDF for a number of years. In the US-1 much of the combat equipment of the PS-1 has been replaced with a variety of rescue equipment and, with the addition of a pair of pockets in the side of the hull to house the main landing gear, the aircraft is amphibious. Normally the aircraft can carry 12 litters for rescue purposes but, when required in an emergency, it can carry as many as 36 litters. Design modifications also

A Japanese PS-1 Shin Meiwa throttles back as it comes in to land. The PS-1 is powered by four Isjikawajima-built General Electric T64-IHI-10 turboprops. It has very good STOL performance and can take off in less than 305 m (1000 ft)

make it possible to use the same basic aircraft type as a water bomber. Its STOL operation capability makes it a very versatile machine. Studies are under way to determine its adaptability as a transport aircraft as well.

Part of the STOL capability is due to incorporation of Boundary Layer Control and a spray suppressor system installed parallel to and about a foot above the chines, from a point almost below the nose radome to a line denoting the plane of rotation of the propellers. The T tail is of modern design and the wing design incorporates the expected ailerons plus outboard flaps which can be connected to the aileron and spoilers plus the BLC, making it a very complex structure. The powerplants of the PS-1/US-1 are four General Electric T64-IHI-10 turboprops of about 3600 hp. These engines are evenly spaced along the leading edge of the shoulder-mounted wing assuring that the air flow from the propellers covers the whole surface of the wing. Wing-tip floats are mounted on V struts midway between the outboard engines and the wing tips.

There continues to be a place in the transportation spectrum which could be best filled by the flying boat, however the money and specialized design personnel are not easily obtained. The three large flying boats currently in production and operation have already been mentioned. These are the Canadair CL-215, the Shin Meiwa PS-1/US-1 and the Beriev Be 12. Some diminutive flying boats of the personal plane category are being constructed such as the Lake LA-4 Buccaneer, the Spencer Air Car S-12D, the Pereira Osprey, the Air Skimmer, the Taylor 'Coot', the Schweizer TSC-1A1 Teal, and the Island Aircraft Spectra IV. To this list can be added conversions which in some cases are nearly total remanufacturing projects. They are installing turboprop engines and the added fuel tankage required to feed them. These projects include the Conroy turbo Albatros, Frakes Turbine Mallard and the McKinnon Turbo Goose and Super Widgeon.

In Japan plans are under way to build a family of flying boats for commercial passenger and cargo service around Japan and probably to other Pacific nations. The largest of these flying boats, to be known as the GS (giant seaplane), will dwarf all others except the Hughes H-4. For a size comparison, the GS is planned to have a span of 256 ft (78 m), the H-4 is 320 ft (97.5 m), but this difference can be accounted for by the greater efficiency of the GS wing requiring less area. A preview of this wing technology is currently in use on the Shin Meiwa PS-1, manufactured by the company that is now preparing the preliminary engineering and economic studies for the pioneer Giant Seaplane.

A Light Amphibian (LA) in this group will probably bear a strong resemblance to the present PS-1/US-1 since discussions have already been held with one operator about a passenger-carrying variant of the PS-1.

Between these two sizes it is planned to develop a medium seaplane (MS) and a medium amphibian (MA). Even the medium amphibian is expected to be impressive with a passenger load of up to 400, about the capacity of a Boeing 747.

It will be interesting to see how these plans develop since they are the only designs of large flying boats now under serious consideration.

Artwork Index

Picture Credits

Atelier Brugman 28
Boeing Airplane Co 103
British Airways 92
Bundesarchiv 83
Canadair 119
Convair 84
Dornier 108, 109
General Dynamics 2
Imperial War Museum 20, 32, 37, 76, 80, 89
John Batchelor 57, 59, 66, 75, 78, 83, 98
John Topham 96, 107, 116, 121, 122
Louis S Casey 4, 8, 14, 35, 40, 54, 57
Mary Evans Picture Library 94
Musée de l'Air 18, 57
National Archives 69, 78
Paul H Wilkinson 26
Photri 6, 12, 16, 22, 31, 52
Popperfoto 86, 87, 91, 97, 105, 124
Radio Times, Hulton 90
Shin Meiwa Industry 126
Smithsonian Institution 6, 11, 22, 38, 40, 44, 45, 47, 48, 58, 89, 111, 112, 114, 123, 125
US Navy 23, 24, 25, 27, 73, 100, 101, 102
Vickers 62, 64, 65, 88, 115